Framingham's
Civil War
Hero

To Ed —
With best regards

Fred Wallace

FRAMINGHAM'S
CIVIL WAR
HERO

The Life of General George H. Gordon

FREDERIC A. WALLACE

Charleston · London

THE
History
PRESS

Published by The History Press
Charleston, SC 29403
www.historypress.net

First published 2011

Manufactured in the United States
ISBN 978.1.60949.378.3

Library of Congress Cataloging-in-Publication Data

Wallace, Frederic A.
Framingham's Civil War hero : the life of General George H. Gordon / Frederic A.
Wallace.
p. cm.
Includes bibliographical references.
ISBN 978-1-60949-378-3
1. Gordon, George H. (George Henry), 1825?-1886. 2. Generals--United States--
Biography. 3. United States--History--Civil War, 1861-1865--Biography. 4. Massachusetts-
-History--Civil War, 1861-1865--Biography. 5. United States--History--Civil War,
1861-1865--Campaigns. 6. Framingham (Mass.)--Biography. I. Title.
E467.1.G63W35 2011
355.0092--dc23
[B]
2011024494

CONTENTS

Preface   7

Chapter 1. The Early Years: Framingham Academy to West Point,
    1828–1846   9

Chapter 2. The Mexican-American War and on the Frontier, 1846–1854   15

Chapter 3. A New Career and Gathering Storm Clouds Across the
    Nation, 1854–1860   24

Chapter 4. The War Begins: Building a Regiment, Spring/Summer
    of 1861   30

Chapter 5. Guarding Washington's Flank Along the Potomac,
    1861–Early 1862   39

Chapter 6. Pursuing "Stonewall" Jackson in the Shenandoah
    Valley, the First Battle of Winchester and Gordon's
    Observations on Slavery, Early 1862   45

Chapter 7. General Pope and the Battles of Cedar Mountain,
    Second Bull Run and Chantilly, Summer of 1862   54

Chapter 8. Antietam: A Day in Hell, Fall of 1862   62

Chapter 9. A Break in the Action and New Commands in Virginia
    and at Gettysburg, Late 1862–Mid-1863   71

Chapter 10. The Siege of Charleston and Capture of Fort Wagner,
    Summer/Fall of 1863   79

Contents

Chapter 11. A Futile Episode in Florida and on to the Deep South,
Spring/Summer of 1864   87

Chapter 12. With Generals Grant and Butler in Eastern Virginia,
Fall/Winter of 1864–1865   95

Chapter 13. The Fall of Richmond and Victory at Last,
Spring/Summer of 1865   102

Chapter 14. Final Military Duties and a Return to Civilian Life,
Summer/Fall of 1865   107

Chapter 15. Early Postwar Years, 1866–1872   114

Chapter 16. Peaceful Days in Framingham and Setting the Record
Straight, 1872–1886   119

Closing Thoughts   129
Notes   131
Bibliography   139
About the Author   143

Preface

In June 2010, I was part of a group from the Framingham History Center, composed of staff and volunteers, who gathered to begin formulating plans for the commemoration of the sesquicentennial of the Civil War. As I listened to the discussion, one name stood out as a most prominent personage of this town associated with that era: Major General George H. Gordon. It was apparent that some kind of recognition of the general would be a part of the activities, and I thought perhaps I would write an article for the center's newsletter about him. I assumed this would be a relatively easy task—surely someone must have written his biography by now. The only thing I was able to find was a three-page sketch at the end of Reverend Josiah Temple's *History of Framingham, Massachusetts*, published in 1885.

I began to wonder about the feasibility of doing one myself. The archives of the history center proved to be a source of some material, but not enough to fill a book. At the suggestion of a colleague, I turned to the Massachusetts Historical Society. There I hit a mother lode: more than six thousand pages of Gordon's personal papers, letters, diaries and military records. As I delved through dozens of personal letters, a picture began to emerge of a very complex character. I was hooked!

Born in Charlestown, Massachusetts, Gordon came to Framingham with his mother when he was a very small child, and he grew up here. Although a career in the military took him to the far corners of our nation and beyond, his heart was always here at the family home on the banks of the Sudbury

River. Whether wounded, sick or just exhausted, he would always return here for sustenance and renewal. When the war ended, he lived out his days here surrounded by other family members.

A very private man, he held strong convictions that sometimes embroiled him in controversy, but he always conducted himself with the utmost honesty and integrity. The regiment that he raised and led early in the war, the 2nd Regiment, Massachusetts Volunteer Infantry, was acknowledged to be one of the best-trained and best-disciplined units of the Union army. General Joseph Hooker once said that it had "no superior."

It is ironic that while several other members of his West Point class gained fame in the war, Gordon's own record remains little known even today. The purpose of this work, therefore, is to bring to him the recognition he rightly deserves. I have been aided in this by his own words, for he was an avid diarist, letter writer and author of three books. In many cases, he has provided us with a firsthand account of events. As I pored over those writings, I became fascinated with the man and filled with admiration for his unwavering commitment to the high principles of duty, honor and honesty. If, as a result of my efforts, he receives greater recognition for his many accomplishments, my goal will have been achieved.

No work of this kind would have been possible without the help of many others. First, thanks go to my colleagues at the Framingham History Center: Annie Murphy, director, for her wholehearted support and encouragement in undertaking this project; my fellow researcher extraordinaire, Kevin Swope; our curator, Dana Dauterman Ricciardi; Michelle McElroy, our operations manager; volunteer Marilyn Manzella; and intern Rebecca Camerato.

I also wish to acknowledge the help of the staff at the Massachusetts Historical Society in accessing General Gordon's personal papers archived there. General Leonid Kondratiuk, of the Massachusetts National Guard Museum, provided much assistance. Professor Mary Murphy, retired from the English Department of Framingham State University and former president of the Framingham History Center, was an invaluable resource in writing the manuscript. Thanks also to Jim Parr, of the Framingham Public Schools, for technical assistance, and to Irv Gorman, of the Massachusetts Military Historical Society, for information about that body. Susan Nicholl was of great help in preparing the manuscript.

And above all I wish to thank my wife, Nancy, for her editing, proofreading and critiquing, not to mention the patience she exhibited while I closeted myself to work on this.

Chapter 1

THE EARLY YEARS

FRAMINGHAM ACADEMY TO WEST POINT, 1828–1846

On a summer's day in 1828, a young woman with two small children stepped down from the stagecoach in Framingham Centre, midway between Boston and Worcester. It was Elizabeth Gordon with her sons, Robert Jr., seven, and George, five. Until recently, she had been living with her husband, Robert, in Charlestown, Massachusetts, near Boston, where he was a teacher. They had married in 1821 and were raising their little family. Life was good and the future had seemed bright, but his untimely death a year earlier had changed all of that. Suddenly she was the sole support for herself and the boys. Through some friends, she learned that a private school in Framingham needed a responsible person to manage its boardinghouse. Making sure that their sons had a good education had always been of great importance to the Gordons. The Framingham Academy, founded in 1792, was the oldest establishment of its kind in Middlesex County and had a fine reputation. In fact, students from distant corners of New England, New York City and even Pennsylvania attended it. In order to accommodate them, the school operated a boardinghouse next door to the school building. When Mrs. Gordon learned of the opening, she applied and got the job. She was elated because it would provide her with a modest income, but more importantly, her sons would be allowed to attend the academy tuition-free.

So on this day, she brushed off the dust of the road and walked briskly toward the building at the far end of the Centre Common, looking forward to a promising new life for herself and her little flock. Framingham was to become their home for life.

Framingham Centre in the mid-1800s. Young Widow Gordon arrived here in 1828, with her sons Robert, seven, and George, five, to start a new life at the Framingham Academy. *Courtesy of* Framingham Illustrated, *1880.*

The widow Gordon thrived in her new role, gaining the respect and support not only of the people of Framingham but also of many prominent families from across the state and beyond, whose children came under her care at the boardinghouse. Today we would call it "networking," and in future years she and her sons would benefit from that. She gained a reputation as one who had some special skill in managing young men.[1] George and Robert adapted quickly to their new environment. Of George, the preceptor would later say:

> *As a scholar* [he has] *my entire approbation. He reads the French language with fluency & accuracy, is a good literary scholar, considerably acquainted in the ancient languages, has studied successfully a number of our best Algebras, and understands as well the principles of Geometry.*[2]

Here the seeds of noble character planted in George by his mother were nurtured and developed by preceptors David Fiske, Duncan Bradford, Jacob Caldwell, Rufus T. King and Charles Goodnow, most of whom were young graduates of Harvard College. Moral instruction was as much a part of the curriculum as the academic disciplines. No doubt George was also expected to help his mother with chores around the boardinghouse.

As the son of the matron, he was probably held to a higher standard of behavior than the other students. Josiah Temple, a classmate of his and later town historian, described him thus: "He was not robust; was timid; was averse to athletic sports, and usually kept his own counsels." This rather uncomplimentary evaluation reflects perhaps the role he was cast into here. Temple's words contrast with those of Preceptor Goodnow. The following excerpt from the above letter, written in support of Gordon's application to West Point, paints a quite different picture of the boy: "He is a youth of commanding tallents [*sic*], strong mind, and vigorous constitution, and in the subscriber's intimation well adapted to the course of life which his plans seem to anticipate."

By 1835, Mrs. Gordon's financial situation had improved sufficiently that she was able, with the aid of a loan, to buy a few acres of land along the Sudbury River close to the bridge on what is today Central Street. Eventually she would build a home there that would be the family homestead for almost a century. The house still stands at a spot known as Gordon's Corner. From this point, she was able to take students as boarders into her own home, a much better arrangement for her financially. Still, money was tight and the

The old academy, built in 1836, replaced an earlier structure. The Gordon brothers attended school here. Photo circa 1900. *Courtesy of the Framingham History Center.*

family lived frugally. At times, there were as many as a dozen boys and girls, aged five to fifteen, living with her![3]

Equally important to George's academic training was his social development. He became comfortable and at ease in the company of prosperous and influential people. He developed the style and manners of a gentleman, qualities stressed at the academy.[4] Many friendships made at the academy would prove helpful to him later in life. He was friendly with an older boy in the neighborhood, too—Charles R. Train, who was to become a successful Boston attorney, U.S. congressman, state senator and attorney general of the Commonwealth of Massachusetts. They became lifelong friends. Living next door to the boardinghouse was the family of Eliphalet Wheeler, one of the original owners of carpet mills in this community. His son, Edgar, was another of Gordon's boyhood chums. Life was not all work and study for him, either. He and his friends found time for play. A single line of houses surrounded the Centre Common, and beyond them was field and forest. Between the Common and the river, the boys would gather chestnuts in the fall; they hunted in Colonel Edgell's woods across Grove Street. Every household had a horse or two, and they rode when they could or hitched one to a wagon or sleigh in the winter for joyrides. It was a bucolic life. Years later, from faraway places, Gordon would write home about how he yearned to be back in Framingham.

Gordon showed interest in a military career from a very early age. He first applied to the U.S. Military Academy at West Point in 1838, just after turning fifteen years old. William Parmenter, the local U.S. congressman, conducted interviews of interested young candidates. Gordon impressed him sufficiently that Parmenter submitted his name, even though Gordon was still under the minimum age of admission. They sent a polite response pointing this out and suggesting that he reapply the following year. Undeterred, he applied again and each following year. Letters of recommendation in support of his candidacy were provided by Preceptor Goodnow, the entire board of trustees of the academy and the pastor of First Framingham's First Parish Church (Unitarian), Reverend A.B. Muzzey. In 1842, at the age of nineteen, he finally received an appointment. For the town, it was quite an honor to have one of its own appointed to the U.S. Military Academy. For the family, it also eased the financial burden of having two children in college at the same time. George's brother Robert had enrolled in Harvard earlier.

The Life of General George H. Gordon

Just before Gordon left home for West Point, there were happenings in the family that would have a significant impact on his life in years to come. His mother's sister, Sarah, died suddenly, leaving five children. Mrs. Gordon took the two youngest, Henry B. Scott, age two, and Maria Elizabeth Scott, age eight, into her home and raised them as her own.[5] To them she was always "Mother Gordon." Their lives would be closely intertwined with George's in a future decade.

Elsewhere in the nation during this time, the long-festering issue of slavery was beginning to command more and more attention. Antislavery societies were springing up, especially in the Northeast, but public opinion was by no means unanimous. At an antislavery gathering in Boston in 1835, William Lloyd Garrison had to be rescued by the police from an angry mob bent on lynching him. How much of this debate Gordon was exposed to at the academy we do not know, but it is reasonable to assume that the subject was discussed often. When the country was finally plunged into war, he would carry with him principles shaped here.

It was September 1842 when he said goodbye to his beloved mother, brother and two little cousins, leaving this quiet little New England town for

Young Lieutenant George H. Gordon, soon after graduation from West Point, from a daguerreotype, circa 1846. *Courtesy of the Framingham History Center.*

the rigors of West Point. It was his first experience away from home, and he soon developed the habit of writing frequent letters—something he would continue to do the rest of his life. He had some difficulty adjusting to his new life. The behavior of the other cadets shocked him at first. In one of his first letters to his mother, he wrote, "This is not a very moral place. All of them swear like fury. I shant [*sic*] get into any habit like that I hope."

But he adapted, and in the four years that followed, the boy was transformed into a man. Academically, he was an average student and received his best grades in the subject of infantry tactics. In the course of four years, he compiled a short list of demerits for minor infractions of the rules, such as missing bed check on occasion and being absent at chapel. Among the members of his class he befriended were many who would distinguish themselves in the coming Civil War, men like George McClellan, Thomas "Stonewall" Jackson, George Pickett, Jesse Reno and one upper classman in particular, Ulysses S. Grant, class of 1844. Their paths would cross again. Now twenty-three years old, Gordon graduated in the spring of 1846, ranking forty-third in a class of sixty-three, and was soon commissioned a second lieutenant.

Chapter 2

THE MEXICAN-AMERICAN WAR AND ON THE FRONTIER, 1846–1854

I n the spring of 1846, shortly after graduation, Gordon was home on leave and argued with his mother over his future. She was concerned. It was a turbulent time in the country. War had just been declared between Mexico and the United States, and a long-running dispute with Great Britain over the borders of the Oregon Territory threatened to turn violent as well. She feared for his safety if he pursued a career in the military. The dispute with his mother troubled him. She was strong-willed, and as a child he had always found it difficult to push back, but now he had grown strong himself and had found his own voice. He tried to reassure her that everything would be all right. He soon received orders to report for duty at the army's Jefferson Barracks in St. Louis, and there he was assigned to a unit of mounted riflemen. In a letter home, written soon after his arrival there, the unusual bond between mother and son was evident:

> *How natural it seems to me to be again writing to you, expressing those true feelings and affection I sometimes while at home withheld...The name of Mother and recollection of such a one as you have been to me will ever bear with it a magic spell; in the hours of pleasure it will but increase my joy, and in times of adversity it will be a healing balm to my sorrows. Hear the true words my dearest mother of a truly repentant son. I love you more than life.*[6]

In the same letter, he referred to the financial problems that seemed to dominate their lives. Mrs. Gordon had borrowed funds from neighbor Isaac Stone and was having trouble repaying. George reassured her, "I will send you money enough, my dear Mother, to pay the interest to Stone…With what Robert and I can do, be assured we will pay all our debts, and get along well in the world."

In the weeks that followed, he tried to assure her that he would not be going into harm's way in either Mexico or the Oregon Territory, only to receive the news on November 30 that he had been assigned to a unit of mounted infantry that would soon ship out for New Orleans. A few weeks later, he found himself writing to her from Brazos Santiago, a barren island at the mouth of the Rio Grande, where the U.S. military was amassing men and supplies for an invasion. He described the scene:

> *It seems to me more than probable that human beings never set foot here before it became necessary to establish a military depot at this place in our operations against Mexico…The number of ships all in the employ of the government lying here, makes it look from the sea more like one of our New England harbors than a desolate island. What an expensive and costly quarrel!*[7]

The last comment may be Gordon's reflection of popular opinion back in New England. The war with Mexico was very unpopular among people in the Northeast. By the spring of 1847, he found himself on Mexican soil. He was in command of a squad of mounted riflemen, part of General Winfield Scott's army of ten thousand, when they landed at Vera Cruz. This was the first amphibious landing on foreign soil by American forces. They laid siege to a city that was so poorly defended that it fell within a few days. Over the next six months, Scott and his army would drive Santa Anna and his army inland 250 miles, all the way to Mexico City. Gordon's journal of their advance to the interior of Mexico, culminating in the Battle of Cerro Gordo, read as follows:[8]

[April 9, 1847]
Day 1   15 miles march.

Day 2   Less sand in road. Beautiful road, beautiful bridges. Road covered with cement, supported by solid masonry. Beautiful flowers and finest looking trees. Ranches, deserted and inhabited by fierce looking inhabitants.

Roofs thatched with straw. Marched 12 miles and encamped near another bridge, larger than other. Beautiful stream, quite a large village near here.

Day 3   To National Bridge.[9] Beautiful flowers and trees as we ascend. Jalapa[10] is four thousand feet higher than Vera Cruz. National bridge a noble structure, 9 arches, built of stone. Hacienda of Santa Anna here—stone pillars and porches.

Day 4   15 miles to Plaza del Rio—Ascent visible. Change of climate. Great much cooler and more agreeable. Hoards of Mexican—white shirts, straw hats, and white, thin pants—swarthy complexions. Most beautiful specimens of cattle. Noble looking oxen and cows. When we found owners we bought them, when we did not find them, took them, made of [illegible] *cattle into camp, hooked thro' the nose and tied by ropes to the tails.*

Day 5   Gen'l Twiggs[11]—I shall not wait for reinforcements but push on early tomorrow—orders to attack at daylight next day. Order again countermanded that volunteers who had joined us might, lacking sufficient rest, want of which might impair their efficiency. This was April 13th. Recruiting porters during that day. Complete investigation [?] *Last night another order issued for another attack at 12 o'clock at night. Parties moving in different directions, signal of attack a rocket. Carrying works at point of bayonet. Order hardly published when countermanded by Gen. Patterson until arrival of Gen. Scott.*

Day 5   Took 2 prisoners today. 3000 volunteers joined us. Camp in a deserted village. Stone houses and Lancers [?] *barracks —bugs all with a bite or sting in Mexico—ticks and jiggers in bed—many varieties of cactus on road—single stock of cylindrical form—30 ft. height. Again in form of a tree with regular trunk and branches. Yards and hedges impenetrable—made of it—attempt to eat—tongue filled with thorns. Santa Anna is reputed to own all the land. And takes poor tenants for his army. One deserter, pantalloons on, dress cape in his hand fantastical colored, coat in his other hand, he was an artillery man.*

Day 6   Gen. Scott's arrival. April 15. A great many scouting parties out reconnoitering with Engineer Officers. I just returned from a reconnaissance behind a stone—in range of their guns, made a [illegible] *fortifications on different eminences.*

Day 7   April 16th Preparations for a decisive action.

Day 8   April 17th Started on road that had been cut. Attacked on emerging.

Thus began the Battle of Cerro Gordo. The Mexicans were dug in on high ground, with three peaks providing commanding views of the road through these mountains. A young captain of the Army Corps of Engineers named Robert E. Lee, scouting the area, found a hidden route up and over the mountains and put men to work cutting a trail. Using this trail, General Scott's forces were able to bypass the Mexican positions on the high ground and attack their unprotected flank and rear. It was a slaughter. The Americans triumphed over a much bigger force, and the Mexicans fled in disarray. It was a major victory.

Graphic depiction of the Battle of Cerro Gordo in the Mexican-American War, April 17–18, 1847, in which Gordon was slightly wounded. *Courtesy of the Library of Congress, LC-USZ62-47992.*

Twiggs's division, of which Gordon's unit was part, had led the attack. Gordon himself was slightly wounded—just a scrape, really. The following day, he walked about the battlefield and saw the bodies, dead and wounded, of Mexicans and Americans, with missing limbs and skulls broken open— the true face of war. He heard the screams as he passed the surgeon's tent:

> *My heart bled for one poor little fellow of my regiment. His arm was shattered by a cannon ball and he was injured otherwise in the breast. The surgeon had taken his arm off at the shoulder. Around him many sufferers, but by his side a friend who stayed to watch and do all he could to alleviate his sufferings. I heard his friend ask kindly if he could do anything more for him. No said he, I feel better now and died. I turned away and thought if this be glory it is enough of it.*[12]

For a young man of twenty-five, this must have been a traumatizing experience. The estimated casualty count for Mexicans was 1,000 killed or wounded and 3,000 made prisoner. Americans had 415 killed or wounded. Gordon made a fine sketch of the battlefield showing the placement of the Mexican forces, the route the Americans took to outflank them and so on. He received a battlefield promotion to first lieutenant for his bravery in this engagement. He showed a certain artistic talent when he made this drawing of the battlefield at Cerro Gordo. In it he showed the trail, discovered by Lee, that allowed U.S. forces to outflank the enemy's superior position.

Over the next four months, Scott's army drove all the way to Mexico City, and in mid-September, vastly outnumbered, they conquered the city. Gordon and his men took part in numerous battles along the way. By now he was a seasoned combat veteran. Lessons learned on these battlefields—the importance of training and discipline—would serve him well in the future. Once hostilities ended, he had some time to acquaint himself with his surroundings and to sample Mexican culture. He was not impressed. In a letter to his friend Edgar Wheeler back in Framingham, he wrote:

> *Would you like to know what kind of a place Mexico is? I can hardly tell you, but believe it to be the most immoral place in the world. Sunday is entirely disregarded, the amusements for last Sunday were a horserace in the morning, a bull fight in the afternoon, and theatre at night. Pretty state of morals, sure enough.*[13]

The war was a disaster for Mexico. A treaty was imposed on the nation that dictated that its entire territory from California to Texas be ceded to the United States. However, U.S. forces continued to occupy Mexico City while negotiations went on, and the troops had to be supplied. This was done by wagon trains that traveled the national road between there and Vera Cruz, some 250 miles away. The countryside was in a state of near anarchy, and the trains were easy targets for bands of irregulars and bandits unless accompanied by military escort.[14] Gordon's unit was often called on for this duty. On one such trip, they were attacked, and he found himself in close, hand-to-hand combat with two guerrillas. His men succeeded in driving them off, but Gordon suffered serious wounds. This incident happened about January 1848. The treaty of peace was concluded in February, and U.S. forces were soon on their way home.

Gordon's regiment returned to its base at Jefferson Barracks in St. Louis but soon was on the move again. In early '49, it was assigned to frontier duty at Fort Vancouver, a remote outpost located on the banks of the Columbia River in the Oregon Territory.[15] However, Gordon did not go with it. He was granted leave for sickness, probably because he was still recovering from the wounds suffered in Mexico.

What a joyous scene it was when he walked into the family home in Framingham. His mother must have been overcome with emotion, for she had not seen her beloved son for more than two years. His little cousins, Maria and Henry, must have been dazzled by their dashing young war hero. Henry, now about nine years old, probably decided then and there that he would be a soldier when he grew up. Maria, or Lizzie, as they liked to call her, now a young lady of fifteen, perhaps could not help feeling some romantic attraction toward the handsome young uniformed officer. The three of them could not now know how intertwined their lives would become in future years. Under his mother's loving care, Gordon regained his health, and he returned to active duty after a few months. Before rejoining his regiment, however, he attended a cavalry school for several weeks, probably harboring hopes of joining this elite branch of the army, perhaps with a promotion as well. But that was not to be.

Eventually, he was ready to rejoin his unit, but this was not going to be an easy task. He first had to travel by steamer from New York to the east coast of Nicaragua—a trip of several thousand miles. From there smaller steamers carried him up the Rio San Juan. This was followed by a trek over the Continental Divide by mule and on to Realajo, a port city on the Pacific

The Life of General George H. Gordon

An 1845 pencil sketch of Fort Vancouver, Oregon Territory, with Native Americans in foreground, by Lieutenant Henry J. Warre. *Sketches in North America and the Oregon Territory (1848), courtesy of the Library of Congress, LC-USZ61-496; LC-USZ62-5407.*

coast. Another steamer trip of about two thousand miles brought him to San Francisco, where, by a strange coincidence, his brother Robert was living, drawn by the gold rush.[16] The two shared a brief reunion, after which George embarked on the final leg: a boat trip north along the coast into the mouth of the Columbia River and one hundred miles upstream to Fort Vancouver—a journey of seven long weeks!

For many years, Fort Vancouver had been a settlement operated by the Hudson's Bay Trading Company. It was a place where the native peoples traded furs for goods and trappers could be resupplied. Once the United States and Great Britain settled their border dispute, our army established a base, and it became the only government presence in the region. It was wild country, populated only by scattered tribes of Native American peoples and a few British trappers. Now, as American settlers began trickling into the region, frictions developed. An ugly incident, known as the Whitman Massacre, happened about this time.[17] There was an uprising in which missionaries Marcus and Narcissa Whitman and a dozen of their helpers were slaughtered. It became the army's job to step in and quell such rebellions. This was the world in which Gordon now found himself. He marveled at the majestic mountains, cascades and forests of Oregon but was beginning to feel uncertain about a career in the military. In his diary, he wrote:

Sunday, November 3rd, 1850. At last in Oregon, and here I have been more than a month at Fort Vancouver, one hundred miles from the mouth of the

Columbia River. I have again entered upon my military duties and with no prospect of change, am breathing out my youth in this desolate spot. I [?] solve the problem of life's purposes, alone in my tent. I have ample time to reflect & examine the Philosophy of nature.[18]

These were not the words of a man who was confident about his future. He began to think of other possibilities, perhaps the practice of law.

However, soon he received exciting news. In the same diary on March 25, 1851, he wrote, "Ordered to the States with the regiment. Is it not a dream? What shall not time unfold?" Unfortunately, what unfolded was a series of lackluster duty assignments: Fort Leavenworth in Kansas, then Kentucky, the Indian Territory of Oklahoma and even a tour as an army recruiter in Texas, but still no promotion! It was time to reevaluate his goals and career. In August 1853, he took a six-month leave of absence[19] and went home to sort things out. We can assume that there were long discussions with his mother and brother, as well as with others.

By now his brother was clerking with Charles R. Train, the family friend and schoolmate from the academy who had a successful law practice in Boston. Train may have encouraged Gordon to pursue the same course. He was leaning toward resigning his commission but decided to give the military one more chance. Returning to duty in March 1854, he was detached from his unit to the Army Corps of Engineers, for which he worked on the coastal survey for a few months. That was the final disappointment. After much deliberation, he made the difficult decision to leave and submitted his resignation in October 1854.

It is interesting at this point to compare Gordon's career path during these years with that of his classmate George B. McClellan, as there are parallels but also dramatic differences. As classmates at West Point, they both were immediately caught up in the Mexican-American War and had similar combat experiences. Both resigned their commissions in the regular army at one point. However, the similarities end there. After the Mexican-American War, Gordon was sent off to the frontier to toil in anonymity for several years, whereas McClellan got a choice position at West Point and was in the mainstream of the military establishment. He received plum assignments, one of which was to survey possible routes for the transcontinental railroad. He was attached to the military academy, for which he wrote army manuals and translated foreign works on military tactics. During this time, he developed a close acquaintance with Jefferson Davis, then secretary of war. Through Davis, McClellan was appointed to be an international observer of the Crimean War and went to that part of the world for a period of time. Upon his return, he wrote a treatise on the conflict. At about the same time, 1855, he was transferred to the cavalry and promoted to the rank of captain. Gordon attended cavalry school, too, but was not successful in transferring branches. Like Gordon, McClellan became frustrated with the peacetime military and resigned his commission in 1857. Using his knowledge and experience in surveying railroad routes and his political connections, he was able to land a choice job as chief executive of the Baltimore and Ohio Railroad. Gordon opted for a career in law.

The contrast between the two could not be more dramatic: Gordon, a man of the highest integrity but more reserved in manner, quiet yet strong-willed; McClellan, a more outgoing personality, more assertive. Gordon, stuck in a far-off post on the frontier, puzzling over his future; and McClellan, mingling in the power circles of Washington, confident of his future. In many ways, their future wartime destinies would reflect their basic human characteristics.

Chapter 3
A NEW CAREER AND GATHERING STORM CLOUDS ACROSS THE NATION, 1854–1860

Gordon, now thirty-two years old, moved to an apartment on Beacon Street in Boston and took up the study of law at Harvard. His brother Robert had done the same a few years earlier and, after clerking with their friend Charles Russell Train, had opened his own practice. Gordon soon found that he had come home to a nation in turmoil. The issue of slavery was tearing the country apart. In the North, the abolitionist movement was gaining strength, especially in Massachusetts, and Framingham played a role in these developments.

Beginning in 1846, every year on Independence Day, the Massachusetts Anti-Slavery Society held a gathering of like-minded people from across the state and beyond at Framingham's Harmony Grove, a popular park with picnic grounds and amusements on Farm Pond. In 1854, an estimated two thousand supporters converged on the Grove. The list of speakers was impressive. It included such notables as William Lloyd Garrison, Sojourner Truth, Henry David Thoreau, Wendell Phillips and Lucy Stone. Each one rose in turn to rail against the institution of slavery. The final speaker was William Lloyd Garrison, and after a particularly fiery speech, he shocked the audience by taking a copy of the U.S. Constitution from his pocket and putting a match to it. His actions made the headlines in newspapers far and wide. It is quite possible that Gordon attended one or more of these gatherings.

Congress seemed powerless to resolve the slavery issue. In 1850, it had passed the Fugitive Slave Act, which gave bounty hunters the right to track

NO SLAVERY!

FOURTH OF JULY!

The Managers of the

Mass. ANTI-SLAVERY SOC'Y

Invite, without distinction of party or sect, ALL who are ready and mean to be known as on LIBER-
TY'S side, in the great struggle which is now upon us, to meet in convention at the

GROVE IN FRAMINGHAM,

On the approaching **FOURTH OF JULY**, there to pass the day in no idle glorying in our country's lib-
erties, but in deep humiliation for her Disgrace and Shame, and in resolute purpose---God being our
leader--- to rescue old Massachusetts at least from being bound forever to the car of Slavery.

SPECIAL TRAINS

Will be run on that day, TO THE GROVE, from Boston, Worces-
ter, and Milford, leaving each place at 9 25 A. M.

RETURNING---Leave the Grove about 5 1-2 P. M. FARE, by
all these Trains, to the Grove and back,

FIFTY CENTS.

**The beauty of the Grove, and the completeness and excellence
of its accommodations, are well known.**

EMINENT SPEAKERS,

From different quarters of the State, will be present.

Earle & Drew, Printers, 213 Main Street, Worcester.

An 1854 broadside for an antislavery rally at Framingham's Harmony Grove. *Courtesy of the Massachusetts Historical Society. Full citation in bibliography.*

down escaped slaves in the free states, seize them and return them to their masters in the South. This enraged the abolitionists. Next, in 1854, Congress passed the Kansas-Nebraska Act. For many years, Congress had maintained a delicate balance in numbers between free and slave states by admitting new ones two at a time and maintaining an artificial boundary, the Mason-Dixon

Gordon, circa 1860, when he was practicing law in Boston. *Courtesy of the Framingham History Center.*

line, between the two regions. But new territories west of the Mississippi were beginning to be settled and didn't fit neatly into this pattern. Under the terms of this legislation, these two large areas, lying north of that imaginary boundary, were put on the path to statehood. The act stipulated that the settlers themselves would determine whether they were to be free or slave states. The possibility that they could become slave states would upset the delicate political and geographic status quo.

Instead of solving the problem, the act made things worse. Kansas became a bloody battleground. Radical abolitionists like John Brown and his followers armed themselves and set out to block the introduction of slavery there by any means, including force. They were followed by groups from Missouri equally committed to slavery's establishment there. The result was inevitable: violence that culminated in the murder of settlers on both sides of the issue.

In 1856, at the nation's capital, Senator Charles Sumner of Massachusetts gave a fiery speech opposing slavery, which so infuriated some Southerners that one of them, South Carolina congressman Preston Brooks, attacked Sumner on the floor of the Senate and beat him senseless. The Supreme Court further exacerbated the situation with its *Dred Scott* decision, which stripped free blacks in the Northern states of U.S. citizenship. Such was the backdrop against which Gordon had reentered civilian life. Talk of secession by Southern states was beginning. Gordon knew that if the situation led to secession there would be war, and his sense of duty would compel him to return to service.

The Life of General George H. Gordon

In Framingham, much was happening during these years. Gordon was beginning to notice that his young cousin Maria, or Lizzie, was growing into a beautiful young woman. As cousins, they were close, but no thought of romance ever crossed his mind. Upon his return to civilian life, he was reintroduced into the social circles of Framingham and Boston and often wished that he had an escort. Lizzie was a ready-made solution to that problem. Lizzie's brother Henry, or Harry, was growing up, too. He was now enrolled at Harvard College. With Robert and George's financial help, Mother Gordon had been able to pay off her mortgage, settle her other debts and was now aging gracefully in the family home at the corner of Edgell and Central Streets.

During this time, Gordon rekindled his friendship with Charles R. Train, a boyhood neighbor. In fact, it is very likely that Train allowed him to clerk in his office before passing the Massachusetts Bar in 1857. Train had shown a real inclination for politics and had a reputation as a skilled lawyer, with offices in both Boston and Framingham. He had already served two terms in the Massachusetts Great and General Court and another as district attorney. Later he would be attorney general of the commonwealth. In the coming days, he would introduce Gordon to many men of power in the halls of the statehouse.

Senator Henry Wilson of the neighboring town of Natick, who served in the U.S. Senate from 1855 to 1873. He was a friend and political ally of Gordon. Throughout the war, he chaired the powerful Senate Committee on Military Affairs. *Courtesy of the Library of Congress, LC-DIG-ppmsca-26560.*

In the neighboring town of Natick, Henry Wilson, a successful businessman who owned a shoe factory and who was an ardent opponent of slavery, decided to enter politics. He was elected to the U.S. Senate in 1855 and served there until 1872, when he became Ulysses S. Grant's running mate in the 1872 presidential election. Being from neighboring towns, he and Gordon were acquainted, and Wilson would prove to be a valuable ally in the future.

During the late 1840s and early '50s, the nation's political parties had fragmented badly under the pressures of the slavery question. Out of the several existing parties—Whigs, Democrats, Free-Soilers and Know-Nothings—there emerged a coalition of more or less antislavery factions that called themselves Republicans. Charles Train joined their ranks and served as a delegate to their first convention in June 1856. There he made the acquaintance of a young man from Illinois named Abraham Lincoln. Although the Republicans failed to win at the national level that year, they made inroads in Congress, as well as in state and local races.

Here in Massachusetts, Republican Nathaniel Banks was elected governor. Neither man could know it at the time, but Gordon's and Banks's fortunes would be closely linked in the coming war. Train was also an ally of Banks's. In 1860, John Andrew was the Republican candidate. He was an ardent abolitionist, and although he was not Train's first choice for governor, Train sponsored a big rally for him at Harmony Grove during the campaign. It is likely that Gordon attended the rally, as this would have been a great opportunity to meet and greet the people of power in state politics. Andrew won easily.

In the midst of such turbulent times, Gordon found himself trying to start a law practice. He rented space in a building on Court Street in Boston, just a block from Charles Train's and close to the seats of power in the statehouse. He still maintained his residence in Framingham, however.[20] The train system was well developed here by the 1850s, and he was a commuter. In the winter, he probably took a room in the city, but home was always at Framingham. Civilian life was beginning to look promising, yet something was missing. He found himself at times longing for the army life, the camaraderie and the structure. The military was still in his blood. He found an answer: the state's militia would satisfy his yearning.

Almost every town in the commonwealth had at least one volunteer militia unit. For the most part, these were loosely organized and not well trained.

Under Massachusetts law, they chose their officers by election from their own ranks. Consequently, officer candidates curried favor from the troops, and discipline tended to be very lax. However, in Boston, there were several elite units with names such as the First Corps of Cadets, the National Lancers, the Fusiliers and the New England Guards Battalion. Their histories dated back to the Revolution and/or the War of 1812. Generally, the ranks of these units were made up of well-educated young gentlemen of the city with time and means, for they had to pay dues to support the units and purchase their own uniforms. Here Gordon could be a soldier, if only part time, and the militia would be a great place to make professional contacts. These elite units also had much more military organization and discipline than most other militia units. Their duties were largely ceremonial, but still they drilled and trained in the use of small arms, light artillery and so forth and marched in parade during holidays and special events. Sometimes they served as the governor's honor guard. Gordon joined and, with his background and experience, rose quickly through the ranks. By the time John Andrew took office in January 1861, Gordon was a captain in the New England Guards.

In the fall of 1860, the Republicans succeeded in electing their man, Abraham Lincoln, to the presidency. This was an affront to the South, and before Lincoln could take office in December, South Carolina's state convention voted to secede from the Union. Several other states quickly followed suit, and the country was on a slippery slope toward disunion.

Upon taking office in January, John Andrew was already aware of the seriousness of the situation, and he did not shrink from the challenge. He put together a team of experienced and knowledgeable men to advise him on the best methods for getting the militia into a better state of readiness. Among them was Captain George H. Gordon of the New England Guards Battalion. A good relationship developed between the two men, and it was said that Gordon's opinions carried much weight with the new governor.[21] Gordon was promoted to the rank of major. The success that had eluded him in the regular army was beginning to unfold.

Chapter 4
THE WAR BEGINS

Building a Regiment, Spring/Summer of 1861

War became a reality on April 12, 1861, when the Confederates fired
on Fort Sumter in Charleston Harbor. While many in the North were
caught up in patriotic fervor, Gordon understood the gravity of the situation.
The following scene took place in his Court Street office the next day:

> *On Saturday, the 13th day of April, 1861, tidings of the attack on Fort
> Sumter came to Boston. On that day, E.R. Mudge, R.S. Fay jun., Greely
> D. Curtis, A.B. Underwood* [Train's law partner], *and others were in
> consultation with George H. Gordon, an educated and experienced soldier.
> "You must give up everything now," said Major Gordon, addressing Mr.
> Underwood, "and prepare for the war. Get men ready. Go to drilling. Get
> yourself ready and give up everything else."*[22]

Most of these men were destined to become officers in Gordon's regiment.

Two days later, President Lincoln sent out a call to the states' governors
for seventy-five thousand militia, to be activated for ninety days. Surely
this would be a brief affair, people reasoned. Governor Andrew's earlier
preparations positioned Massachusetts to react quickly. Companies of
militia descended on Boston. On April 17, the governor stood before many
of them on Boston Common and bid them Godspeed as they prepared to
board trains for Washington. Most knowledgeable military men were aware
that these units were ill-prepared for what lay ahead. Gordon had been
thinking of a different approach—to raise entirely new units from scratch,
modeled after units of the regular army. He had in mind four criteria. First,

the men would have to enlist for the duration of the war. Second, the senior officer alone would have the authority to select his junior officers based on such qualifications as military experience, education and moral character. (He strongly opposed the current practice of men choosing officers by election from their own ranks.) Third, as he put it, they should be men filled with "the impulsive ardor of the morning of life." Finally, there would be strict military discipline and training as in a regular army unit. His experiences in the Mexican-American War had taught him that there was no substitute for these.

On April 15, Gordon presented his proposal to the governor. After a brief consultation, Andrew threw his full support behind it and promised to use his influence to get the backing of Washington because, at present, no provision existed under law for such a unit. Gordon dispatched two of his close associates, Wilder Dwight and George Andrews, to travel to Washington and present his plan to the War Department. On April 30, approval was granted.

Others in the War Department must have recognized the merit of Gordon's approach and shared the same concerns about militia units, because on May 3, the president issued an order calling for the raising of thirty-nine regiments, or forty-two thousand men, to serve for three years or the duration. Soon after, the War Department issued rules governing the selection of these units' officers that closely resembled Gordon's criteria. There was one very important difference, however: the final authority for the selection of officers was placed in the hands of the governors. Thus, the seeds of a future conflict between Andrew and Gordon had been planted.

In Framingham, the news of the fall of Fort Sumter was met with a swift response. The town immediately began raising and equipping a company of militia, and at a town meeting early in May, the following resolution was adopted:

> *Whereas a grave and extraordinary emergency now exists; whereby the security of our beloved government is threatened by a portion of the people, who are bound and sworn to support, defend and obey it; and whereas in the prosecution of its designs, the rebellious portion have resorted to the employment of armed force; have unlawfully and forcibly seized and do now hold much property belonging to the common government, and do generally disown and set it at defiance; and whereas the citizens of this*

town do profess and are ready to maintain our unswerving loyalty to the government, obtained by our fathers by the sacrifice of their blood and treasure, and handed down to us as a sacred and inestimable gift, under which we have enjoyed those blessings which make life happy—we have assembled together this day to take such measures as are in our power to assist in preserving and maintaining for ourselves and our children this goodly heritage.[23]

Gordon's regiment was chosen to be one of eight that would be activated from Massachusetts under this presidential order. By May 20, the ranks of his regiment—ten companies of one hundred men each—were nearly full. Gordon was officially commissioned colonel and commanding officer. Through a bookkeeping twist in the statehouse, Gordon's unit was designated the 2nd Regiment, Massachusetts Volunteer Infantry. This always rankled him; he wanted it known that he was first, and years later in his personal memoirs he went to great lengths to document the fact that *this* regiment had been the *first* accepted by the president! The governor recommended several individuals whom he thought were officer material. For now, there was a spirit of cooperation between the two men, and Gordon accepted them.

For his troops to train, they found a perfect location: the old Brook Farm in West Roxbury. This property had been the site of a utopian transcendentalist community but had been vacant for some time. On May 11, the first units arrived, and the regiment began to take shape. The training camp was given a new name, Camp Andrew, to honor the governor.

In the weeks that followed, Gordon began the arduous task of molding his raw recruits—both enlisted men and officers—into soldiers. For officers, he had chosen many of the men he knew from the elite Boston militias, in particular the New England Guards Battalion. For his second-in-command, he picked George Andrews. Like Gordon, Andrews came from a family of modest means. He had graduated from West Point in 1851 and, like Gordon, resigned in 1855 to seek a better future for himself. Currently, he was working in Boston and was a member of the New England Guards. When war broke out, he heard of Gordon's plans and immediately joined him. Together, they worked the men hard and soon earned reputations as tough taskmasters, drilling the men for long hours late into the evening and demanding strict discipline.

Another of the men chosen for officer's rank was Wilder Dwight. This young man had no military background but otherwise fit all of Gordon's

Young Lieutenant Robert
Gould Shaw, an officer in
Gordon's 2nd Regiment,
Massachusetts Volunteer
Infantry, 1861. *Courtesy of the
Library of Congress, LC-DIG-
ppmsca10890.*

criteria for officer material; bright, young, Harvard-educated and of the
highest moral character, he was eager to join the Union cause. In the legal
community of Boston, he had established a reputation as the most promising
young man of his profession. At the outbreak of the war, he set everything
else aside to serve in the military. Gordon would make him a company
commander. Dwight was destined to die on the battlefield at Antietam.

Still another bright young man put in command of a company was
Robert Gould Shaw. A son of one of America's wealthiest families at this
time, he had spent his youth in leisurely pursuits, traveling and studying
in Europe. In 1856, he enrolled in Harvard College, where he became
acquainted with Henry B. Scott, Gordon's young cousin. The two were
members of the class of 1860. After graduation, he went to work in the

family business in New York City and, while there, joined an exclusive militia regiment, the 7th New York National Guard. Once the war began, he came to Boston intent on enlisting and signed up with Gordon's 2nd Massachusetts. He immediately took a liking to the military life and, under Gordon's tutelage over the next twenty-two months, became a well-trained officer and was promoted to the rank of captain. In a letter home, written in December 1861, Shaw praised Gordon:

> *We hear that Col. Gordon is likely to be made a Brigadier. There is not a man in the regiment, I believe, who will not be very sorry, not to go into action with him. As far as we can judge, he is a man who would be cool and clear-headed in a fight. He has, besides, the affection of the men, and, when he takes hold, can make them do what he chooses.*[24]

Shaw would rise to the rank of colonel and go on to achieve fame as the commander of the 54th Regiment, Massachusetts Volunteer Infantry, the first all-black regiment in the Union army. He, too, was killed on the field of battle, at Fort Wagner, South Carolina.

One evening, during training at Camp Andrew, Gordon passed by the tent of one company officer, Captain Whitney, and noticed that he was sharing a glass of spirits with one of his sergeants. To Gordon, this was an egregious breach of military discipline—one of the regular army's basic rules was the prohibition of fraternization between officers and enlisted men. Whitney's actions smacked of the old militia that Gordon so disliked. He demanded the captain's resignation on the spot and forwarded it to the governor with his own approval attached. The governor pushed back, urging Gordon to reconsider. He also encouraged the man to withdraw the resignation, reasoning that he had been a good militia officer and just needed time to adapt to the army's new rules. Gordon would not budge. In a face-to-face interview with the governor, Gordon defended his position, and harsh words were exchanged. In the end, although he did not agree, Andrew accepted the resignation in the interests of good order in the unit. But he was not happy, and news of this dispute got into the press and became very public. The governor felt rebuffed by Gordon and embarrassed by all the press. Relations between the two soured.

By the end of June, Gordon was pleased with the progress that his young officers and men had made. When he was satisfied, a ceremony was arranged to celebrate the occasion by "receiving the colors," according to

The regimental flag, presented to Gordon and his regiment on July 1, 1861, as they prepared to leave for the front in Virginia. *Courtesy of the Commonwealth of Massachusetts Art Commission, cw-02c-1987.363.*

military tradition. On the twenty-sixth, they gathered in parade formation on the grounds of their encampment. The ladies of the Regimental Aid Association had made a beautiful flag of silk, with stars of gold thread embroidered on the field of blue. Atop the shaft was an eagle of solid silver. Thousands of dollars had been subscribed by private citizens to outfit and support the regiment until the federal government would take responsibility for its support, and many of those contributors attended. The *Boston Daily Advertiser* described the scene:

> *The regiment was drawn up in line of battle, and presented a fine and soldierly appearance. Their movements all indicated a high state of efficiency and drill. A large number of spectators, including the donors and their friends, were present on the hill overlooking the parade ground. At a quarter past five, Mr. E. Francis Bowditch advanced towards Colonel Gordon, before the line, unfolding the colors to the breeze. The battalion saluted by presenting arms, the band playing the "Star Spangled Banner."*

The officers having been ordered to the front, gathered in a group around the colonel and were addressed by Mr. J. Lothrop Motley, on behalf of the ladies presenting the flag:

Colonel Gordon, Gentlemen and Ladies: To your hand, Colonel Gordon, to your tried valor, to your signal ability, to your fortunate military experience on the field of honor, we gladly intrust these our most precious possessions, the bone and muscle of our most ancient Commonwealth, and the aspirations and the ardor of the youthful chivalry of our State.

We know that in your hands, and in those of your brave companions in arms, the welfare and honor of the whole country are safe. Our hearts are too full for words. Our hopes, our prayers, our pride—everything but our fears—go with you. In the name of your countrymen, I present to you this flag. We know that its folds will never be stained, that they will ever wave foremost among the foremost where duty and honor call.

As I place it in your hand, I will only add the brief and simple phrase of the herald in the early days of warfare and chivalry, "May God defend the Right!"

Colonel Gordon then replied substantially:

"Sir, In the name of the Second Regiment of Massachusetts Volunteers, it becomes my duty to receive this magnificent flag, and to respond as well as I may. I could wish that someone more eloquent might answer for them. But this is not the hour or the place for words.

"When I look upon this long line of men, eager to fight for their country, and in the youthful but resolute faces of these officers who surround me, I feel a deep sense of the responsibilities on which I have entered, and which, God willing, I will discharge. This flag of our country, which bears on its folds the glorious record of the war of the Revolution, of the war of 1812, and of another conquest of Mexico has never been trailed in the dust before a foreign foe. It was left to our own countrymen to make the first record of its dishonor. But it still continues the flag of our country, and, God willing, none other shall wave defiantly before it. Never, till it was struck down, did we feel it to be so truly the symbol of our country's greatness. We had been accustomed to regard it in times of peace as only a symbol of our prosperity; but now that the hour of trial has come, we look to it as the emblem of our

freedom and our power. It shall never cease to wave over our whole country.

"We accept this flag, and will render our account of it hereafter. And, Sir, borrowing the sentiment of that immortal statesman, we will strive to defend it so that not a star shall be removed nor a stripe erased."

At the conclusion of the colonel's address, the officers returned to their posts. The color guard advanced, received the colors from Mr. Bowditch, and carried them to their position in the line.

On July 1, the regiment would receive its state militia colors, and soon after, on the sixth, came orders from Washington to report to General Patterson at Williamsport, Maryland, and thus began its service. On the eighth, the men broke camp and boarded trains. Before departing, Gordon wrote home:[25]

> *Monday Morning,*
> *July 8, 1861*
>
> *My Dear Mother,*
> *I am in great confusion as you may well suppose. But yet I have a moment which I must write in pencil. I shall write from N.Y. Now I see that I am discharging my duty to you, my dear Mother, as well as to my country, and my God. You shall be advised of my movements. Love to Lizzie. I will write her.*
> *Your affectionate son,*
> *George H. Gordon*

A group of Gordon's young officers: Adjutant John A. Fox, Captain Daniel Oakey, Captain William E. Perkins and Captain F.W. Crowninshield, 1861. *Courtesy of MOLLUS-MA.*

Three days' travel by train, steamer and foot brought them to their destination, where they soon crossed the Potomac and stepped onto enemy soil in Virginia for the first time. "The officers were in full uniform with epaulettes and sashes. The ranks were full, a thousand men, marching in close order, moving with the military precision of veterans, and keeping time to the music of a full band, which echoed through the streets,"[26] Gordon wrote. Riding astride his horse at the head of the column, Gordon felt a glow of pride and satisfaction at what they had achieved in such a short time. It was a good beginning, but he knew that there was suffering and sacrifice ahead.

Chapter 5
GUARDING WASHINGTON'S FLANK
ALONG THE POTOMAC, 1861–EARLY 1862

The protection of Washington, D.C., was one of the Union forces' primary concerns during the first weeks of the war. In this regard, the Shenandoah Valley was of great strategic importance. A glance at a map of the area makes the reasons clear. The valley is like a giant conduit connecting the South and West to Washington and the Northeast. If the Confederates controlled it, Washington would be under threat of attack from those directions. On the other hand, if Union forces could seal it off, the city's northwest flank would be protected. The Confederates had put a small army into that area under the command of General Joseph E. Johnston,[27] and they were thought to be dug in at the town of Winchester. A Union force of about twelve thousand, led by General George Patterson, was positioned at the mouth of the valley and along the Potomac. Its mission was to block any enemy advance from that direction.

Gordon and his regiment became part of Patterson's force, and their first assignment was to take the town of Harpers Ferry, situated at the entrance to the valley. As they approached, they found that the enemy had withdrawn, and the town was taken without opposition. About this time, a rumor began to circulate around camp that Patterson was to be replaced by a new commander, General Nathaniel Banks, a name familiar to Gordon. He was the former governor of Massachusetts. The rumor proved to be true, and Gordon was appalled. Surely Banks, a man with little education and totally lacking military experience, would not be made a major general and entrusted with the lives

New York Volunteer militia at Harpers Ferry, summer of 1861. Gordon's regiment was stationed nearby. The site of a Federal armory, Harpers Ferry changed hands several times during the war. Gordon and his men passed through here three times. The town can be seen in the distance. *Courtesy of the Library of Congress, LC-USZ62-72761.*

of thousands of troops? It was hard for Gordon to swallow, but a good soldier does not question such decisions and carries on. And that's what he did.

The Union forces only partially succeeded in keeping the valley sealed off, and in late July, Johnston and his men slipped away to join General Beauregard at the little town of Manassas, just twenty-five miles outside Washington. A battle was looming and Washington panicked. Union leaders gathered as many troops as they could muster—about thirty-five thousand—to oppose Beauregard and Johnston's thirty-two thousand men. This developed into the first major engagement of the war, known today as the First Battle of Bull Run (or Manassas), which took place on July 21. Both poorly trained and ill-equipped, the armies hurled themselves at each other with terrible losses. At the end of the day, the Union forces were driven from the field in defeat. Gordon and his men were miles away and did not see action.

Things were off to a bad start for the Union. General Winfield Scott (now in his mid-seventies), the same Scott who had led U.S. troops (including

Gordon) into battle in Mexico fifteen years earlier, had been in command of all Union forces up to this time. After Bull Run, the president, the War Department and the cabinet worked feverishly to put together a functioning army. They brought in a new man, Major General George B. McClellan, Gordon's old classmate. One of their greatest needs was qualified officers to train and lead the thousands of raw recruits and ill-prepared militias. As a West Point graduate with combat experience, Gordon was a logical candidate for higher rank, perhaps general. The authority to commission men at that level rested solely with the president. Names could be submitted by the governors or the Senate Military Affairs Committee. Gordon had influential friends in Congress, including Senator Henry Wilson of Natick, who was chairman of the Senate Military Affairs Committee, and Charles Train, then a congressman. In August, they submitted his name for a brigadier generalship, and in early September he was summoned to Washington for an interview with the president. Lincoln commended him on his qualifications, asked a few questions and, after a pause, said that he could not heed this recommendation "because the Governor of your State protests against it."[28] Andrew had intervened.

Sorely disappointed, Gordon returned to his duties with the Army of the Potomac. Banks had enough confidence in Gordon to give him command of a brigade[29] even without the promotion. He was now commanding, in addition to his own unit, the 5th Connecticut, the 19th and 20th New York, the 46th Pennsylvania and a Rhode Island battery of artillery —in all, nearly five thousand men. He tried to contain his bitterness, but in a letter to his mother he let it all out:

Oct. 7, 1861:
I am well and inspired to work for the best ends…In charge of a Brigade of 5 regiments (tho' John A. Andrew protests against it) and a battery of artillery. In introducing changes in discipline, drill and cleanliness in camp life, I find much to do. I give all this my personal attention, visiting the several regiments twice a day, often drilling the men myself, attending to hospitals and tasks to men and Officers to drill and guard duty. I see manifest improvement. I have the pleasure of knowing that the various regiments respect their commander and that they are improving under my command. I have all the responsibility, all the position, but not the rank and not the pay, thanks to John A. Andrew, the Philanthropist.[30]

The feud continued. In the following weeks, Gordon had several vacancies to fill in his regiment and sent names up to Andrew for approval. Andrew rejected them. Then Andrew sent Gordon names of persons he wanted commissioned. In turn, Gordon replied that he could not accept them until he could thoroughly evaluate the men. Back and forth it went, with Gordon trying to assert his authority under the original agreement he had with the governor and Andrew asserting his authority based on the rules expounded by the War Department. As winter approached, the armies retired from the battlefield. The weather simply made warfare impossible. Gordon and his men moved to the outskirts of Frederick, Maryland, and settled into winter quarters. He was able to take leave to be home for Thanksgiving. Visitors from home sometimes came to visit the troops during these lulls. One such visit by a group of businessmen from Boston included E.F. "Frank" Bowditch, the future owner of Millwood Farm in Framingham—and the same person who had presented the colors to the regiment the previous June. The two men shared a love of horses and later became close friends.

On the homefront, there was much activity associated with the war. The women of Framingham were organizing auxiliary units of the U.S. Sanitary Commission, a forerunner of the Red Cross. No doubt Mother Gordon and Lizzie were rolling bandages and knitting socks for the troops in one of these groups. In Boston, the Regimental Aid Association, made up of wives, mothers and sisters of the men of the 2nd, were hard at work making socks

Graphic depiction of the 2nd Regiment, Massachusetts Volunteer Infantry, encamped in winter quarters near Frederick, Maryland, winter of 1861–62. Brook Farm to Cedar Mountain, *opposite page 88.*

and undergarments for the men. Young cousin Henry had graduated from Harvard and was enrolled in law school, but he wanted to do his part in the war effort and had asked George to help him get a commission. In fact, his was one of the nominations that Governor Andrew had rejected! In a letter to Gordon, Henry wrote, "I can't stand being at home when I could be useful with you or with some other regiment."[31] Later, he wrote again:

Cambridge, Dec. 11, 1861

My Dear George,
You will have received before this the Govr's letter informing you that he has appointed Oakley and Dalton in place of the men you nominated. I called there this afternoon and the reason he assigned or rather one of the aids was that these men had been waiting much longer than we.[32]

Gordon's great coat, part of the uniform he wore throughout the war. On display at the Framingham History Center Museum.
Photo by Austin Daniells.

And again in January:

> *The Gov'r & Aids have promised me the next vacancy and say they are daily expecting official notice thereof, and that I am sure of it. Accordingly I have ordered my uniforms and shall try to come on with Fox on Monday or Tuesday. I have seen Mudge and it would be very pleasant to me to be in his Company, because I should have to live with Bob Shaw,[33] whom I know so well.*[34]

On January 16, he received his commission and joined Gordon's regiment as a second lieutenant. Brother Robert was living at home now after struggling unsuccessfully to establish a law practice in Boston. Family members wrote to Gordon, expressing concern that he seemed to be suffering from a malaise (what we might call depression today). Gordon wrote to him urging that he shake off whatever was weighing him down and offering to help in any way he could. He even suggested that Robert come to Maryland and spend some time with him there. As far as it is known, the offer was not accepted.

Back in Maryland, Gordon and his men used the time to rest, regroup and repair their weapons, and the winter passed uneventfully.

Chapter 6
PURSUING "STONEWALL" JACKSON IN THE SHENANDOAH VALLEY, THE FIRST BATTLE OF WINCHESTER AND GORDON'S OBSERVATIONS ON SLAVERY, EARLY 1862

S pring came early to Maryland, and by March the armies were on the move again. Gordon's destiny continued to be linked to that of Banks. Still a colonel, he found himself in command of a brigade once again. Union forces in the East had been consolidated into the Army of the Potomac under the command of Major General George B. McClellan. The threat from the Shenandoah Valley was still of great concern, and Washington wanted it cleared of all Confederate troops. McClellan tasked General Banks with the job and gave him three divisions (the 5th Corps) amounting to about thirty-eight thousand men, including Gordon and his men.[35] On February 27, they broke camp, crossed the Potomac once again and soon encamped at Harpers Ferry. They now faced a new Confederate commander, Gordon's old classmate General Thomas "Stonewall" Jackson, who was operating in the valley with a small force of ten thousand. Other Confederate troops nearby could join him on short notice as well. Banks began a cautious advance up the valley toward Winchester. During this time, there was a chance meeting between Gordon and McClellan, and the two "had a pleasant and familiar conversation for an hour and more."[36]

Banks moved his force toward Winchester, reaching the outskirts on the eleventh. Expecting to encounter resistance, they were surprised to find that all was quiet. They took the city without firing a shot. Jackson and his force had withdrawn just the day before. In the weeks that followed, one of the most famous campaigns of military history, the Valley Campaign, took place here. Jackson and Banks played a dangerous game of cat and mouse. Banks would advance; Jackson would feign and attack and fall back, retreating farther and farther into the valley. Banks would follow, each time bringing vast quantities of supplies in great wagon trains that slowed his movements.

On March 25, just beyond Winchester, Jackson attacked one of Banks's divisions at Kernstown but was beaten and retreated farther into the valley. It was a small victory for Union forces, but it buoyed their spirits. Banks continued to follow, experiencing frequent skirmishes along the way through the town of Strasburg and beyond—further extending his supply lines.

As the Union force approached the head of the valley at Harrisonburg, Jackson and his forces seemed to disappear. They were nowhere to be found. Assuming that they had given up the fight and departed, Banks set up his headquarters behind the front line at Strasburg, amassing all the supplies there. Gordon, in a forward position, commandeered the home of an elderly lady for his headquarters. He noticed that her slaves lived in quarters even more squalid than most. One day, as he rode by, he encountered a young woman standing by one of the huts. As he often did, he engaged her in conversation, telling her that she was now free and could go in search of a better life if she so chose. A conversation followed:[37]

She: "*I'm going with you!*" [Gordon wrote in the vernacular.]
He: "*Very well, come along.*"
She: "*But I can't go without my child.*"
He: "*Then bring it with you.*"
She: "*I can't. I haven't got her.*"
He: "*Where is she?*"
She: "*Over there at Miss _____. She has her.*"
He: "*Go and get her then if you have the time.*"
She: "*She won't give her up to me.*"
He: "*What shall I do? I have no time now to send.*"
She: "*You just give me a 'writing,' and I'll go with it.*"
He: "*That won't do you any good; our troops are all leaving here; the people won't mind our writings.*"
She: "*Yes it will. You just give me writing.*"

Her name was Peggy. Gordon quickly grasped the situation. The girl was accustomed to a system in which she and her baby were nothing more than

Slaves in Virginia, much as Gordon would have encountered them in the early days of the war. He corresponded with Ralph Waldo Emerson on the subject of slavery, relating conversations he had with "this species of property." *Courtesy of the Library of Congress, LC-DIG-cwph-01005.*

property and that a bill of sale, or "writing," would be needed to secure her release from the owner. Gordon scribbled out an order on a sheet of paper and gave it to her, and off she went. He left to attend to his duties and soon forgot about her.

At this time, Gordon and the rest of Banks's army were preparing to return to Winchester, having received intelligence that Jackson had left the valley to join Lee's army. Washington ordered two of Banks's divisions to redeploy to the south in support of McClellan. With Jackson gone, they reasoned, a single division would be sufficient to control the valley. Unfortunately, their intelligence was wrong. In fact, Jackson had crossed over the mountains to an adjacent valley and was swinging around and in back of their force. Banks had no idea what was happening. His army began to retrace its steps back toward Strasburg, unaware of Jackson's movements.

As Gordon's unit started its return, he rode along beside his column. Suddenly, he spied Peggy running beside the wagons and marching men, her child on her shoulder and a large bundle slung across her back. He described the scene:

Telling her to come to my camp when we halted for the night, I rode on, pondering on the amazing changes which time works in the field of human events; upon the fleeing fugitive, hiding in swamps and tracked by bloodhounds, to the fugitive fearless in the presence of ten thousand bayonets, glistening in the hands of ten thousand hated abolitionists—for this is practically what we had become.[38]

Gordon kept her on as a cook throughout the rest of the campaign. When they were back in Maryland, he gave her money and put her on a train to Boston to start a new life as a free person, probably a domestic in the home of someone he knew.

While Banks's withdrawal got slowly underway, Jackson was busy. He had linked up with General Richard Ewell, and their combined force amounted to about seventeen thousand men. Banks had fewer than ten thousand at his disposal now. With superior numbers and the element of surprise in his favor, Jackson decided to go on the offensive. On May 23, a very agitated orderly rode into camp at Strasburg seeking General Banks. He brought news that Jackson had defeated a small Union force near Front Royal and was on the march toward Strasburg.

Banks was slow to respond to the situation. With his battlefield experience, Gordon understood the danger and tried to alert Banks, who steadfastly refused to take action.[39] More disturbing reports were received: Front Royal had fallen. Finally, orders were given to move back to Winchester. Banks put one of his brigadiers, John Hatch, in charge of coordinating a rear-guard action and ordered a hasty retreat. The single road out of town became hopelessly clogged with men and wagons filled with tons of supplies, rations, ammunition and weapons. Jackson then struck, turning the scene into chaos. Gordon did what he could to protect the retreat and regroup Union forces in his area. Unable to locate General Hatch, Gordon assumed command on the field.[40] With his own brigade, one other and some cavalry, he organized an effective rear-guard action that slowed Jackson's advance. Approaching Winchester, they were able to set up a defensive perimeter and make a stand that prevented total disaster. Many of the supplies that had been on the road were torched to prevent them falling into enemy hands, but much more was abandoned intact as well. Jackson's men had a field day pillaging—so much so that their forward movement was slowed.

Banks was not on the battlefield. They reached Winchester in the early hours of the twenty-fourth. The next day, the Union forces made a hasty retreat back to the Potomac, leaving many men captured and wounded, as well as tons of supplies. On the twenty-sixth, they recrossed the river to the safety of the Maryland shore. Jackson and his troops were satisfied to enjoy the spoils of war and stayed in Winchester. The 2nd Massachusetts had its first taste of real warfare and had done well. The whole affair was a black eye for Banks. The Confederates dubbed him "Commissary Banks," because of the huge quantities of supplies he had provided them.

These events became known as the First Battle of Winchester. Gordon's performance was recognized as exemplary by his colleagues. The general officers involved in the affair sent a letter to the War Department:[41]

Williamsport, Md., May 31, 1862

To the Hon. Edwin Stanton, Secretary of War,

The undersigned officers of the army, serving in the Department of the Shenandoah, take great pleasure in recommending for the appointment of brigadier general, Colonel George H. Gordon, commanding Second Massachusetts Regiment.

Colonel Gordon for the last three months filled the position asked for him, having been in command of the Third Brigade of Williams' division. The high state of discipline attained by his brigade, together with its admirable drill, have proved his competency for the position.

The appointment is more particularly asked as a reward for the military skill and good conduct shown by him at the battle of Winchester on Sunday last, and throughout the retreat from Strasburg to this place.

N.P. Banks, M.G.C.

John P. Hatch, Brig. Gen. Cav'y *S.W. Crawford, Brig. Gen., U.S.V.*
A.S. Williams, B.G.C. 1st Div. *Geo. S. Greene, Brig. Gen. U.S.V.*

The War Department sent a telegram to Governor Andrew informing him that it could no longer delay Gordon's promotion, and in a letter from the adjutant general's office dated June 12, Gordon received notice that he had been commissioned brigadier general of the U.S. Volunteers. Soon after, he received a cordial letter of congratulations from the governor. Gordon was vindicated.

While these events were taking place in the Shenandoah, Union forces under McClellan had embarked on a major campaign to take Richmond, the capital of the Confederacy. The Peninsula Campaign, as it came to be known, began at the end of March. Tens of thousands of troops were moved by ship down the James River to the Union stronghold at Fortress Monroe, where they began a slow advance inland toward Richmond. For two and a half months, they advanced up the peninsula, engaging in several battles until they were within six miles of Richmond. When Rebel commander General Joe Johnston was wounded, a new man, General Robert E. Lee, took over. Through a series of brilliant moves, Lee set McClellan's forces back on their heels. By the end of June, the Peninsula Campaign had ended in failure, and McClellan and his forces were recalled to Washington. More bad news for the Union.

Throughout the Shenandoah campaign, a small force of Confederate cavalry led by Colonel Turner Ashby had been a terrible distraction to the Union forces. Ashby tormented them with lightning raids, destroying supplies, killing and capturing men and tearing up railroads, bridges and more. Their horses were far superior to those of the Union. After one skirmish outside the little town of Woodstock, troops of Gordon's regiment found a riderless horse, saddled and bridled, that had belonged to one of Ashby's men. Gordon saw it and ordered it brought to him. The story of this horse is told in his own words:

> *Having occasion towards night to visit General Banks at his headquarters, distant about three miles, I called for this horse, jumped on his back, and let him take his own gait. Though it was a still night, I found, from the way the air was rushing past my face, that my horse must be going at great speed.*[42]

It was a magnificent animal. In a bit of battlefield one-upmanship, Gordon named him Ashby. He went on:

> *His weight was over eleven hundred, and his height in proportion to his weight. His nostril was of enormous size; his ear was of large size, but well made and expressive; his tail was handsome and full; his mane soft but not thick, though slightly flowing; his color was a dark bay, with a black streak running from his mane down his back to the roots of his tail… From the day of his capture, until the close of the war, that horse was my inseparable companion. Nothing could tire him or break his spirits…I have never known such a horse. I never expect to know one like him. Every*

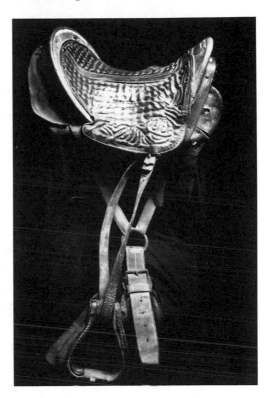

Gordon's saddle. Called a "McClellan," it was standard issue for Union officers. It's on display at the Framingham History Center Museum. *Photo by Austin Daniells.*

moment a manifestation of power and gameness, fearless in his sweeping gallop, unmoved by the din of battle, his mettle inspired courage.

Gordon seldom involved himself in the politics of the day. However, he corresponded at least once with Ralph Waldo Emerson, the great philosopher and transcendentalist, on the issue of slavery. It was in April 1862, just after Union forces had given "Stonewall" Jackson's men a small but significant beating near Kernstown, Virginia. Gordon happened to read Emerson's treatise, "American Civilization," in *Atlantic* magazine and wrote him the following letter:[43]

Camp near Edenburg, Va
April 8ᵗʰ, 1862

My dear Sir,
    Stealing a moment from military duties, I have just read your paper on American Civilization in the Atlantic for April—[44]

Nine months of military service in the slave states of Maryland and Virginia has developed facts showing the feelings of this species of property,[45] as it is termed at the south. What I hear from slaves may not be uninteresting to you. Firstly I find no exceptions to their manifestations of joy at sight of our columns. The mansion of the slave owner is generally closely shut, apparently vacated in minutes of our march. From the rough cabins of the negroes salutations are waved. We are hailed as deliverers. I have sought opportunities of conversation with slaves, male and female, intelligent and stupid—I have never found one contented. All think our mission is to free them, and some have so far meditated as to see difficulties in the way. Said I to a stupid looking girl of about sixteen, at the home of whose master I passed the night—Do you know what we are here for? "I 'specs you's here to free us." Do you want to be free? "I does." Don't you like your master? "No Sir." Why? "He sold my mother once." When? "Twelve years ago." But your master looks like a kind man, and treats us kindly (my brigade of three thousand men had surrounded his premises to encamp for the night). "I know he looks so but he 'buses me." How? "He ties me up and whips me with a cow hide." This conversation was drawn out in no presence but mine, and in tones inexplicably sad. I have never found but one word to express my conviction of their own feeling; hopelessness, utter despair. Again, and as more [?] practical, while following up in pursuit of defeated rebels from Winchester[46] my Officers and staff were taking breakfast at the home of a Virginian near Strasburg. The proprietor's apparent cordiality was induced by fear. While at table we were waited on by a bright looking yellow woman about twenty five years of age. When her master had left the room, I questioned her of the rebels—she spoke intelligently but hurriedly and in low tones as if desiring to communicate with us and yet afraid her master would overhear. She told me among other things that the rebel General Jackson took breakfast at that house the day after his defeat, that her master asked him to make another stand, that he Jackson expressed doubt as to the result should he do so. This she overheard while standing at the door. I then asked her if she liked to live with her master. "No Sir." Then why do you? "Where shall I go?" Go north. "What will I do with my family and how shall I have my friends? We can't all go. And how can we be separated? I thought it would be best for me to wait for the law." What law? "Why the law that is going to be passed to set us free." I could make no answer to this. "What would you

52

advise me to do?" she said, as I arose to leave the room. Wait a little while and see what is done for you I replied.

The affection of these poor creatures for each other binds them together, and the freedom which one member of a family may possess by their own act but renders them and those they leave behind miserable enough. Besides, the slaves do not want to leave this country, they know no other, here they were born, here they wish to die. The blacks are our faithful friends and as against the rebels of the south [as we]. They can be trusted; information secretly lodged in the hands of a poor black by a friend in the rebel army, pencil marks on a scrap of paper, hid away and handed me as the last fugitives of the flying rebels were in sight of my advance, I received as I entered the town.

I could, Sir, fill many sheets with sad stories and criminal outrages narrated by this unoffending people. But I have already taken a liberty which is only excused by my sympathy with your article in the Atlantic—

Apologizing for the liberty,

I am, Sir, with great respect,
Truly yours,

Geo. H. Gordon
Col. 2nd Mass. Reg't
Comdg 3rd Brigade

R.W. Emerson
Concord
Mass.

He received a warm reply from Emerson, who expressed his gratitude for the letter and agreed with Gordon's conclusions on the subject. The Emancipation Proclamation would not be issued until eight months later.

Chapter 7
GENERAL POPE AND THE BATTLES OF CEDAR MOUNTAIN, SECOND BULL RUN AND CHANTILLY, SUMMER OF 1862

On June 26, Banks received notice of a major shakeup in the army. Until now, all forces in the East had been part of a single entity, the Army of the Potomac, under the command of Major General George B. McClellan. Now those forces north and west of Washington were to be consolidated into a separate, new command, the Army of Virginia, under a new commander, Major General John Pope. This included Banks's forces. Pope had a reputation as a fighter, and Washington looked to him for a more aggressive prosecution of the war in this theater.

Now a brigadier general, Gordon had to relinquish direct command of his 2nd Massachusetts but was able to make it part of his brigade. He lobbied successfully for his subordinate, Colonel George Andrews, to be given that command, with the rank of major, and he brought several other young men from the regiment with him to form the nucleus of his brigade staff. Henry B. Scott, his young cousin, now joined him as assistant adjutant general with the rank of captain, and the young Boston Brahmin Robert Gould Shaw was made an aide on his staff. Gordon received a warm letter of thanks from Shaw's parents.[47]

On June 27, General Pope visited Banks and his troops. Gordon found him to be a foulmouthed, boastful figure. Pope also bad-mouthed General McClellan, which did not sit well with Gordon. He instructed Banks to keep Jackson off balance but avoid a direct fight, reasoning that Jackson could easily call up reinforcements that would tip any battle in his favor. On paper,

Banks's corps was 14,000, but sickness and casualties had thinned the ranks considerably. He probably could field only about 7,500 able-bodied men. Pope's forces spent most of July rebuilding.

Northern Virginia continued to be a battleground. Each side had several small fighting forces located throughout the area. The Confederates had about twenty-four thousand men; the largest single piece was about fourteen thousand under General "Stonewall" Jackson. Pope's Union forces of thirty-eight thousand men composed three corps led by Generals Sigel, Banks and McDowell. Gordon's brigade was still a part of Banks's corps, and they were all positioned east of the Shenandoah Valley again, protecting Washington's northern and western flanks. It was midsummer, and the heat was terrible. Sickness was rampant among the troops. Gordon described the situation in early August:

> *Diarrhea was more prevalent than usual. The atmosphere of our camp while we were at Little Washington was like that of a pest house, from the number of dead animals lying about. In Augur's division of our corps, two entire regiments had been sent to the hospital. In the 60th New York men died eight and ten a day; in a single day two commissioned officers were buried. The drum and fife constantly sounding the dead march, made the evenings sad and solemn...The Second Regiment suffered but in a less degree.*[48]

Measles were epidemic, but the greatest fear was typhoid fever.

Some small towns in the area were of great strategic importance because they were rail centers and could provide either side the ability to move men, supplies and equipment rapidly. One of these was Culpeper, while another was Gordonsville. Union forces were on a line with Banks in the center, at Culpeper, Sigel and his corps several miles to the west (or right) and McDowell several miles to the east (or left). In mid-July, Jackson advanced and occupied Gordonsville. Now the two armies faced each other, separated by just twenty miles. Two weeks passed with no confrontation.

On August 9, after consulting with Lee, Jackson went on the attack. Weakened by sickness and injury, Banks's force of 7,500 men and thirty artillery pieces was at the center. Jackson had about 27,000 men and sixty artillery pieces. With such an advantage, if Jackson could strike hard and fast before Pope could bring in reinforcements, it would be an easy victory. Then, Lee and Jackson reasoned, they could roll up the separated pieces of

Lieutenant Henry B. Scott, 1862, Gordon's young cousin, who received a commission in January and joined the 2nd Massachusetts in the Shenandoah Valley, as Gordon's adjutant shortly thereafter. *Courtesy of MOLLUS-MA.*

Pope's army, one by one, leaving Washington completely exposed on that flank. It could be *the* turning point in the war.

Banks and Pope knew that they were badly outnumbered at the center and could have opted to retreat and await reinforcements. It would have been justified, given the odds. But Pope was not one to back down from a fight. At some point, the order was given to stand and fight.[49] The source of that order is still in dispute. After Union forces made an initial advance, Jackson counterattacked and drove the entire Union line back. In the fog of war, orders were misunderstood, units got lost and arguments erupted among Union officers. At one point, Gordon received an order, said to be coming directly from Banks, for his regiment to charge across an open field heavily defended by the enemy. Knowing that it would be suicidal, he refused to obey and kept his troops in place. Banks and Pope were nearby behind the lines, giving out orders and apparently unaware of how badly things were going. Furious at their mismanagement of the field, Gordon went to them and let loose, saying, "General Pope, this battle should not have been fought, sir!" To which Pope promptly replied, "I never ordered it fought, sir!"[50] At the end of the day, Union forces were driven from the field and fell back to Culpeper. Jackson chose not to pursue for now and returned to Gordonsville.

Gordon's brigade had suffered terribly: 465 casualties, representing over 30 percent of his total force. Several of the bright young men he had personally recruited to be officers in the 2nd Massachusetts were dead. Overall, Union casualties were 2,403, Confederate 1,418.[51] History would record this as the Battle of Cedar Mountain.

Soon after, Lee and Jackson decided that the time was right to implement their grand plan, but they needed a little time to get Lee's and Longstreet's forces into the area. Now, Pope recognized the danger and made the rational response. On August 18, he ordered a full retreat to the eastern shore of the Rappahannock. The river became the dividing line between the two armies. Over the next several weeks, they probed each other's defenses by engaging in raids and minor engagements. In one such raid, led by the famous Jeb Stuart, Confederate cavalry got behind Union lines. Several of Pope's staff were captured and much of his personal property stolen! He was furious.

In mid-August, Gordon gave a copy of his official report on the battle at Cedar Mountain to an Associated Press reporter. Within a day or two, the report was published in newspapers throughout the North. In it, he was frank and honest about the beating they had taken, and he put the responsibility where he thought it belonged—on Pope. He knew it was against regulations to release the report, and years later he wrote of the incident:

> While I think such acts were reprehensible, I believe that they were not without justification. It was a bad practice, which arose from a necessity to impart the truth about operations...and from a laudable desire to neutralize the falsehoods about others, and the bluster and brag about themselves, which certain officers themselves and one general officer in particular, in Banks' Corps, furnished immediately after the battle of Cedar Mountain to all the dailies in New York and Pennsylvania.[52]

Once again, when Gordon saw injustice or dishonesty, he could not remain silent. He had little tolerance for certain things, such as incompetence in public officials or military leaders, and he despised it when either tried to cover up their own failures by twisting facts or blaming their subordinates. When Pope was told of the newspaper reports, he became so angry that he sent a member of his staff to investigate. Gordon readily acknowledged that he was the source. Pope had him arrested on the spot and relieved of his command. A group of Gordon's fellow officers pleaded with Pope in Gordon's defense, and shortly after, Pope rescinded his order. The whole episode lasted less than twenty-four hours. The next time the two met, Pope made no reference to it, but it put a strain on their relations.

Now the two armies were poised on either side of the Rappahannock River, Pope on the Washington side and Jackson and Lee to the west and south. On the twenty-third and twenty-fourth, Gordon's brigade was engaged in a sharp firefight at a spot on the Rappahannock known as Beverly Ford, where Pope feared Lee and Jackson might try to launch an attack. They successfully repulsed the attack. At the same time, a much more serious situation was developing to the north. Jackson had succeeded in getting his entire force across the Rappahannock without detection. In an extraordinary flanking maneuver, he marched his force sixty miles in two days, bypassed the Union forces and gained their rear at Manassas Junction. Here a very small force was guarding vast stores of Union supplies, including food, equipment and ammunition. They were quickly overrun, and Jackson's men had a field day plundering, burning and generally consuming or destroying anything of value. The material loss to Pope was huge, but the more serious fact was that Jackson had been able to interpose himself between Pope and Washington, cut his lines of supply and communication and expose the capital to attack.

That was on August 27, and it set the stage for the next major battle of the war in the East, known as Second Manassas or Second Bull Run. Pope planned an immediate attack to drive Jackson back. Lee and Longstreet moved to attack Pope from a different direction. With combined forces totaling about fifty-five thousand, the Confederates squared off against Pope's Army of Virginia, which totaled sixty thousand to seventy thousand. Jackson was initially isolated, and Pope turned his full force against him, but Lee and Longstreet were quick to respond. The battle raged over three days, August 28–30.

On the twenty-seventh, while the battle raged at Manassas Junction, Banks (with his forces, including Gordon) was ordered to guard other vast stores of supplies and equipment and start moving them toward Manassas. (Pope must not have been aware of the situation when he gave this order.) Why at this time an entire corps would be devoted to this rather noncritical task in the face of the dire situation Pope faced is not clear. Gordon's frustration at not being part of the action is shown in his own words:

> *To repair bridges and mend highways for the safe passage of horse, equipments, salt pork and hard bread is undoubtedly a military duty. But to send, under the circumstances in which Pope found himself, a whole corps along a road, upon which no enemy appeared, to defend wagon trains, instead of using it to oppose the enemy was an error of judgment, arising from…* [Pope's] *over-caution.*[53]

Much of the material was being transported by train, and Banks's corps followed the rail line of Orange & Alexandria Railroad. He was told to move cautiously toward Manassas. If he could not protect the supplies, he was to

Second Battle of Bull Run, August 1862. Gordon's duties included guarding Union supply trains (rail and wagon) from enemy capture. If they were in danger, his orders were to destroy them. Here Union troops examine the burned-out remains of a supply train near Manassas. *Courtesy of the Library of Congress, LC-DIG-cwpb00260.*

destroy them. Inexplicably, during the next two days—the fiercest of this battle—Banks received no further communication from Pope (according to Gordon's statement). At a place called Kettle Run, they encountered a burned-out bridge that blocked the trains of supplies, so they transferred as much material as possible to wagons and destroyed the rest. So on this most important day of this momentous battle, Banks, with an entire corps consisting of two divisions and perhaps five thousand men, sat idle! On the thirty-first, all Federal troops were in retreat toward Washington. With his army that had been pulled back from Richmond, McClellan tried desperately to resupply and send troops, but it was too little, too late. Banks received orders to destroy any and all supplies under his control and proceed to Centerville, a town near Washington, where Pope had gathered his forces to regroup and organize.

At this point, the Federal force was estimated to be about sixty thousand. Before Pope could fully prepare, Confederate troops again began flanking moves and forced a retreat toward the town of Chantilly. On September 1, outside this small town, there was another clash in which Banks's corps played a small part. At this point, both armies were low on ammunition, lacked food and had had no rest for days. The next day, Pope received an order from Washington to pull his force back to the fortifications around the city, and that marked the end of one of the fiercest battles of the war to date. Casualties amounted to about 10,000 killed or wounded for the Union, and 8,500 for the Confederates.

Everywhere in Washington, signs of defeat were apparent—disorganized units arriving by train, stragglers walking in from the field, the streets filled with ambulances and tired officers looking for hotel rooms. There was an air of panic.

Gordon made his way into the city on September 2 and chanced to meet his old friend, Charles Train. Train was shocked at what he saw. Gordon looked positively disheveled and confided that he had not been out of his clothes for fifteen days. Since Congress was not in session, Train decided that as an able-bodied man he had to do his part. In a letter to his wife, he wrote:

Willard's Hotel
September 4, 1862

My Dear Wife,
I wrote you a hurried letter yesterday. Today has changed all my plans.
Gordon came in all worn out, and without a staff officer left. Of course I,

at once volunteered to go on his staff and give him all the aid in my power.
I did not wish to join him except in a military capacity, because if I should
happen to be captured I could not be exchanged as a civilian.[54]

Train conferred with President Lincoln and requested a temporary commission without pay. With the War Department's approval, his request was granted, and he joined Gordon's staff as an adjutant, with the rank of captain. He would soon know the ugly realties of war.

After this whole sad affair, Pope was quietly reassigned to the western frontier and would not command combat forces again. Banks claimed an illness and was reassigned. Later, President Lincoln put him in charge of a massive recruiting effort in the Northeast, where his political acumen would be useful—and it kept him off the battlefield. But for Gordon and the army, there would be only a brief respite because Lee and Jackson were on the move, and they had an invasion of Maryland and Pennsylvania on the drawing board.

On September 1, during the chaos of the Union retreat, Pope sent a communication to Washington in which he accused some of his generals of being uncooperative. In particular, he named Major General Fitz-John Porter of traitorous behavior by withholding his troops from battle, using delaying tactics and disobeying orders outright. Pope attributed his own defeat to Porter. Porter was just one class ahead of Gordon at West Point, and they had fought side by side in Mexico and in some early actions of this war. They were good friends. Eventually, Porter was put on trial by a military commission, found guilty and dismissed from the army. His career and life were ruined.

Gordon was outraged by what had happened. He saw it as another example of how men in high places often make scapegoats of subordinates in order to cover up their own failures. He was powerless to do anything now, but after the war, exonerating his friend became his life's work.

Chapter 8
ANTIETAM

A Day in Hell, Fall of 1862

Washington did not have to wait long to learn of Lee's intentions. On September 3, elements of Lee's army crossed the Potomac into Maryland, and his entire force soon followed. Pope and Banks were gone, and once again McClellan was the leader of all Union forces in the theater. Not certain of Lee's ultimate target, he first had to protect Washington and ordered elements of Pope's army to occupy ground north of Washington. On the fourth, Banks's former corps, including Gordon and his men, crossed the Potomac into Maryland. Exhausted and hungry, they pushed northward for two days, finally stopping outside Rockville and establishing a line between the capital and Lee's army. Here they were able to get a few days' rest, eat and resupply themselves while other elements of the Union army gathered nearby.

By now, Gordon's brigade, consisting of the 2nd Massachusetts, the 3rd Wisconsin and the 27th Indiana, together with a Rhode Island Artillery Battery, had been together as a unit for several months. They had jelled into a well-coordinated, disciplined fighting team. At Rockville, two regiments composed entirely of fresh recruits, the 13th New Jersey and the 107th New York, were added to Gordon's command. Train was at Gordon's side now. A brigade of five regiments at full strength should have numbered about five thousand, but due to the attrition of battle, Gordon's was considerably smaller. Replacements for men lost in battle were slow. The 2nd Massachusetts, for example, should have been one thousand men at full strength, but at this time it could field fewer than five hundred.

McClellan reconstituted his old Army of the Potomac, merging Pope's troops and his own into three armies: the 1st and 9th Corps, commanded by

General Ambrose Burnside; the 2nd and 12th Corps, led by General Edwin Sumner; and the 6th and 4th Corps, led by General William Franklin. The forces formerly commanded by Banks, including Gordon's brigade, were incorporated into the 12th Corps and, for the moment, had no permanent commander. By September 9, McClellan had massed about seventy-five thousand troops and put them in motion, cautiously moving northward. Lee had a combined force numbering about forty thousand.

Lee's plan was to advance north rapidly, gain control of the Shenandoah Valley (which would become his line of supply) and move through Maryland into Pennsylvania. But in order to do so, he would have to control that valley. But there was a problem: the Union force of about ten thousand occupying Harpers Ferry would have to be eliminated. His ultimate goal was to attack and take Harrisburg, the capital of Pennsylvania. But in one of the most bizarre twists of this war, his plans, known as Special Order 191, fell into Union hands. Now McClellan knew exactly what Lee was planning to do, which provided a huge strategic advantage to him. He could direct his full force northward, leaving just a small garrison behind at Washington. As Lee marched on, he split Jackson off from his main force and sent him west to attack and secure Harpers Ferry. Lee and Longstreet were headed north toward Hagerstown, Maryland, clearing the way for an assault into Pennsylvania, when they got word that their secret plan had been compromised. Lee now had to turn his army around and head south to face McClellan. He sent word to Jackson to rejoin him. By the time Jackson received these orders, he had already taken Harpers Ferry. The Union forces there simply surrendered without a fight. Once again, great quantities of Union weapons, ammunition and supplies fell into Rebel hands. Leaving a small force to hold the city, Jackson quickly marched east to rejoin Lee. The two armies were now on a collision course, setting the stage for a major battle.

A spur of the Blue Ridge, known as South Mountain, stood between them. Passage was by roads or "gaps," as the locals called them. Lee took up defensive positions here, knowing that the terrain would help him stop the Union advance. On September 14, the Union forces reached South Mountain. Burnside's force was thrown against the right, or north, at Turner's and Fox's Gaps. Lee's forces held fast throughout the day but suffered high casualties, and by nightfall they were being hard pressed. Lee ordered a withdrawal.

On that same day, the 12th Corps (Banks's old unit) got a new commander, Major General Joseph Mansfield, a well-respected career soldier. The chain of command above Gordon was now General Alonzo Williams, 1st Division commander, and Mansfield was above him. The next morning, Gordon and the rest of Mansfield's force carried out "mop-up" operations at South Mountain and advanced toward Sharpsburg. During the day, Gordon received the sad news that his friend and West Point classmate, Major General Jesse Reno, had been killed back at South Mountain. It had been a short but bloody battle, with 2,325 Union troops killed or wounded and Confederate losses numbering 325 killed, 1,560 wounded and 800 missing. In the end, it was considered a Union victory. They advanced toward Sharpsburg and Antietam Creek.

The two armies spent the fifteenth and sixteenth jockeying for position on either side of a little stream called Antietam Creek. Lee assembled his forces on the west bank and set up a defensive line there, while McClellan massed his to the east. The creek ran more or less north–south and was about fifty yards wide, spanned by three widely separated bridges. A short distance to the west, a roadway, known as the Hagerstown Pike, paralleled the creek; to the south was the town of Sharpsburg and the Potomac River. Lee's forces were well positioned on high ground with open fields in front, which gave them full view of the creek at their center. The surrounding terrain was a mix of open farmland fields separated by small clumps of woods.

The great battle, which took place on the seventeenth, can be thought of as three distinct actions: Hooker's and Mansfield's assaults to the north on Lee's left flank, which took place early in the day; Sumner's assault on Lee's center, an area that became known as "Bloody Lane," from midmorning to midday; and Burnside's assault on the now famous bridge to the south, which lasted all day, peaking in the afternoon. We'll focus on Gordon's role throughout these actions. Late in the day, or shortly after dark on the sixteenth, Hooker advanced across the creek at the northernmost bridge. Mansfield's 12th Corps (hence Gordon) was assigned to support Hooker and crossed about the same time, encamping for the night at Hooker's rear about two miles from the Confederate lines.

Just before dawn (5:30 a.m.) on the seventeenth, Hooker's forces made the first move, advancing southward parallel and to the east of the Hagerstown Pike. Facing them was "Stonewall" Jackson and his army. The two were about evenly matched, the former having 8,600 men and the latter 7,700. Mansfield's Corps was at the rear, ready to respond when needed.

As Hooker advanced, he reached an open area, which has since become famous as "the Cornfield." It was an open area, 250 yards wide and 400 yards long, surrounded on three sides by woods, referred to later in battle reports as the "East Woods," "West Woods" and "North Woods." In the hours that followed, these would provide cover for troops and artillery firing into the Cornfield. Ahead was an area of high ground with a small white building (Dunker Church) on it. Hooker recognized its strategic value and was determined to take it. As his troops emerged from the North Woods into the Cornfield, they were greeted by a hail of bullets and short-range artillery[55] coming from the West Woods. His advance stalled.

Waiting in reserve, Mansfield's Corps received urgent orders to move forward in support. Gordon swung into action, as did the rest of the corps. He put his three seasoned regiments (the 2nd Massachusetts, the 3rd Wisconsin and the 27th Indiana) in front, formed a line and placed the two new regiments of raw recruits (the 107th New York and the 13th New Jersey) in reserve at the rear. They passed through the East Woods and reached the edge of the Cornfield, intending to aid Hooker. They were met with the same withering fire that Hooker had faced. Leading the charge, Gordon took his men on the attack. Major General Mansfield, riding into the open ground to observe, was mortally wounded and carried from the field. The corps was momentarily leaderless, but General Alonzo Williams quickly assumed command. Now Gordon and the rest of the 12th Corps repeated the process with the same result: neither side was able gain decisive advantage.

Over the next two hours, the Cornfield changed hands repeatedly. One side would charge and advance, only to be met by intense resistance and counterattack and be driven back. The other side would then repeat the process. Soon the Cornfield was strewn with dead and wounded. One officer later described the scene as "artillery hell."

Hooker tried to gather his scattered units together and was himself shot in the foot. Now both the 1st and 12th Corps had lost their commanders. Division-level officers desperately tried to maintain order and restore a line of battle. Sumner's 2nd Corps entered the fray to aid the two beleaguered corps. Williams, the temporary commander of the 12th, regrouped his forces. It was now only about 8:00 a.m., yet they had been fighting for two and a half hours, and already hundreds were dead. Sumner's men fought valiantly, allowing Williams time to gather and reform his 12th Corps. Even as he did this, Sumner's forces, which had advanced some distance, began to be repelled. The regrouped 12th was summoned back into action. Once again Gordon and the others advanced, with Gordon himself commanding a regiment closest to him. Again they were exposed to withering gunfire and artillery. It was at this point that Gordon's dear friend, Colonel Dwight, was hit and fell to the ground, mortally wounded. He would lie unattended on the battlefield for the rest of the day.

Carrying out his duties as a staff aide, Charles Train ran orders here and there. He was transfixed by what he was witnessing. That night, in his diary, he wrote:

> Oh God, oh God, what sights and sounds. I went to the rear of the left wing, Gordon making a most rash but magnificent charge. Wasn't killed, thank God. We were separated in the confusion and did not find ourselves for three hours.[56]

Another part of the 12th Corps (General George Greene's) finally gained the high ground at the Dunker Church. Isolated and outflanked by the enemy on two sides, they withdrew. Eventually, Gordon and the others were relieved by fresh troops of Sumner's 2nd Corps.

The struggle went on until late morning. There was heavy fighting along and across the Hagerstown Pike as well. In the end it was a stalemate. Exhausted, the two sides withdrew. Gordon's old regiment, the 2nd Massachusetts, had casualties amounting to about 27 percent of its total force on the field. The 3rd Wisconsin and the 27th Indiana suffered even higher losses. For the time being, they retired from the field of battle, took care of their wounded, resupplied themselves and awaited orders.

Action shifted to the center of the Confederate position, where a sunken road would become known as "Bloody Lane." More terrible action occurred here, but Gordon and the 12th Corps were not involved. He said in his report:

> The services of my brigade during a portion of the remainder of the day were confined to forming a supporting line to fresher troops in our front… Again, however, late in the afternoon, was I called into action, a direct order addressed in person from General McClellan to my brigade, to support General Franklin in his intended movement to the front upon the disputed woods [Eastern Woods].[57]

Battle of Antietam, September 17, 1862, and the aftermath along the Hagerstown Road. Confederate dead lie along the fence near the Cornfield and Dunker Church, where Gordon's regiment battled forces led by Generals Jackson and Hood. *Courtesy of the Library of Congress, LC-DIGcwpb-01097.*

They spent the night drawn up in a line of battle to the rear of Franklin's forces and saw no further action.

Elsewhere throughout the entire day, Burnside's forces had been attempting to launch an attack on Lee's southern or right flank position, across the stream at the southernmost bridge. The Confederates, however, had a superior defensive position on a ridge overlooking the bridge. With each Union assault, their sharpshooters cut them down like ducks in a shooting gallery. Attack after attack failed. Finally, late in the day, Burnside's forces gained a foothold on the west side and prepared to advance. At that very moment, Confederate reinforcements arrived. It was the force that Jackson had left at Harpers Ferry, and many of them were dressed in captured Union blue uniforms. In the assault that followed, this created great confusion, and the Union forces were driven back to the bridge.

Along the entire Confederate line, their forces were now spread so thin that one more massive attack would have resulted in a complete rout. In fact, McClellan had the troops to do it. He had two full corps, Porter's 5th and Franklin's 4th, both of which had remained in reserve all day. But ever cautious, McClellan opted to cease the attack, and the battle was over at 5:30 p.m. on the seventeenth.

Burnside's Bridge, so-called, at Antietam Creek circa 1862. Confederate sharpshooters positioned on high ground to the west (left in photo) had a clear view of the bridge and turned back wave after wave of Union soldiers attempting to cross from the right (east). *Courtesy of the Library of Congress, LC-DIG-cwpb-01133.*

In one day, the Union had suffered more than 12,000 casualties, with 2,108 dead. The Confederates had suffered more than 10,000, with 1,546 dead. It would be the bloodiest single day of the war. Gordon's brigade was typical: he lost 620, killed or wounded. Most of the dead and wounded were left where they lay overnight. The Union commanders fully expected McClellan to order a hot pursuit. Instead, the next day an eerie calm settled over the area. The Confederates stood in place, while both sides attempted to gather up their dead and wounded. The numbers were staggering. After dark on the eighteenth, Lee organized a withdrawal of all his forces across the Potomac and into Virginia.

Train and Gordon walked the Cornfield and the woods surrounding it. The dead lay row upon row, as if in formation. At the sunken road, it looked like a regiment was in position there, except they were all dead. Train wrote in his diary:

> *Sept. 19th, the enemy have left during the night. Rode over into their lines. The stink was awful. I vomited an hour. They have not buried their dead. I vomited an hour and thought I should die. I went to all the hospitals and went to B___ to take care of Dwight. Arrived in time to see him die. A good and brave man. Gordon sent me to Frederick [Md.] to telegraph. Will leave to go to Washington if I can get there.[58]*

He had seen enough of war. He would return home after this.

The Life of General George H. Gordon

We return briefly to events just before the fighting had begun. As Gordon had ridden past his ranks, checking their readiness in the first light of dawn, he noticed his young officer and friend, Colonel Dwight, sitting astride his horse with pen and paper in hand. He inquired what he was doing. "Oh, I am writing to my mother,"[59] Dwight replied. Gordon nodded approvingly. Then the order to move out was given, and Dwight put the unfinished letter in his pocket. Hours later, he was mortally wounded near Dunker Church and fell from his horse to the ground. As he lay there, unattended, he found the strength to finish the letter. Later, when he was brought off the field to a hospital, he gave it to a friend, who saw that it was delivered. His mother preserved it:

[Written before battle:[60]]

Near Sharpsburg, Sept. 17th, 1862
In the field

My Dear Mother,
    It is a misty, moisty morning. We are engaging the enemy and we are drawn up in support of Hooker, who is now banging away most briskly. I write in the saddle to send you my love and to say that I am well so far.

[Written as he lay wounded:]

I am wounded so as to be helpless. Goodbye—if so it must be. I think I die in victory. God defend our Country. I trust in God and love you all to the last. Dearest love to Father and all my dear brothers. Our troops have left the point of the field where I lie.

Truly yours,
Wilder

All is well with those who have faith.

He lingered on for two days. The death of this bright and promising young lawyer from one of Boston's socially prominent families was a shock to the community. Gordon himself was deeply grieved by this loss.

This was a great turning point in the course of the war, and Gordon and his men had been at the forefront through it all. Things had not gone well for the North up to now. People of the North had been growing restless and discouraged with the slow pace of the war, but now they had something to cheer about. Lee's attempt to invade the North had been thwarted. On the twenty-third, Lincoln issued the Emancipation Proclamation. Up to now, the war had been about the interpretation of the Constitution and internal insurrection. Now it had become a moral issue: slavery.

Today, visitors to the Antietam Battlefield National Park will find, at a site near the old Hagerstown Road, a plaque that commemorates Gordon's role in the fight that took place there.

Chapter 9

A Break in the Action and New Commands in Virginia and at Gettysburg, Late 1862–Mid-1863

In the days immediately following Antietam, the 12th Corps, including Gordon's brigade, moved a few miles south to Maryland Heights, across from Harpers Ferry, and awaited orders to cross into Virginia in pursuit of Lee's army. The Rebels had been badly weakened and were vulnerable. A swift pursuit on the Union's part probably would have overwhelmed them. McClellan had fresh troops in reserve ready to go but did not give the order. As he had done so many times in the past, he hesitated, became overly cautious and did nothing.

It was just about a year since the 2nd Massachusetts had encamped at the same spot on Maryland Heights, and to the men it probably felt as though nothing had been gained. In Gordon's words, "It would be vain to deny that at this period there was a despondent feeling in the army. After all the sufferings and reverses the end seemed no nearer."[61] Days extended into weeks, and still the order to pursue did not come. Lincoln became more and more impatient. A month passed. On the one hand, it was an opportunity for the Union armies to rest, resupply themselves and bring in fresh replacements for the thousands of men who had been lost. But it allowed Lee to do the same. Finally, in the last week of October, McClellan got moving again, crossing into Virginia—but at a snail's pace.

Washington had had enough. On November 7, McClellan was *again* relieved of his command, and Major General Ambrose Burnside took his place. Burnside had been just a year behind Gordon at West Point, and they had fought side by side in Mexico as well. Burnside took on his new role as commander of the Army of the Potomac, reorganized and prepared to launch new attacks, setting his sights on Fredericksburg, Virginia, as a steppingstone on the road to taking Richmond.

The new movement of the Union army into Virginia had begun on October 27, but Williams's division of the 12th Corps was detached and stayed in place to guard the upper Potomac. This included Gordon's brigade. They were now refreshed and feeling more optimistic, even eager to get back into action. But it was not to be for now. They were assigned to guard the stretch of river running about ten miles on either side of Sharpsburg. Gordon moved his men a few miles northward again and set up his headquarters in that city, after arriving on November 13.

Here camp life settled into a routine. The men began to build little shelters, and the camp took on the appearance of a shantytown. Gordon made sure their days were not spent in idleness. They drilled, drilled, drilled. They identified defensive positions and threw up earthworks. Patrols were set up along the shores of the river. In their spare time, they occupied themselves with amusements such as horse racing, contests of strength, games and so on. Sutlers (traveling peddlers) set up shop outside camp and sold little items of comfort, such as tobacco and candy. Alcohol could be had, but Gordon was very hard on anyone caught selling or using it.

The weather was changing now. Nights were becoming colder, and men often lacked blankets and warm clothing. Gordon's quartermaster did what he could to get supplies, and back home the Regimental Aid Association, made up mostly of the wives and sisters of the men, many from Boston's most prominent families, were busy making packages for the troops containing "woolen undershirts, drawers, socks, and articles of that substantial kind." Gordon had written to them complaining that the items provided by the government were "thin, flimsy things, poorly adapted to guard against the inclemency of the season."[62] On Thanksgiving, the troops were able to "find" local goods, including turkeys, chickens and pigs, to supplement their regular rations. Some of the local ladies sympathetic to the Union cause brought them baked goods and such. They managed to have quite a feast.

Officers, on the other hand, were almost always well fed. Most of them were people of some wealth, and each one had a retinue of staff besides military aides and adjutants. Typically they brought cooks, servants and one or more wagons with personal belongings and food. For quarters they would commandeer a dwelling near their encampments, with or without the permission of the owners, and make themselves at home. They frequently gathered for elaborate banquets when conditions allowed. Gordon described such a scene:

> *And then came social dinners. Of which none could compare with those given by the surgeon of the brigade, in his excellent dining hall (a hospital tent), and his selection of wines—not supplied we would remark, by the Christian or Sanitary Commission…Impatiently expected and long awaited the dinner hour arrived…bringing in due course before admiring eyes and palates soups which tormented the appetite, bouille's wonderfully seasoned and garnished, an immense Bologna sausage reclining upon a dewy head of cabbage and hashed turnip, roasts of mutton, chickens undecapitated, quails, apples stuffed, peaches and puddings, over which last, from utter dissolution of appetite, only sympathetic sighs could be breathed…With coffee the entertainment closed. Of the sherry which introduced it, of the wine which was interspersed through it, and of the real Havanas which followed it, of these and of the impressions a sense of the fullness of the feast created, no utterance of appreciation was possible. It only remained to endeavor to repay the attentions.*[63]

Thanksgiving passed and the weather turned wintery. It was the custom for armies to stand down and settle into quarters during this season, but there was unrest in the North. The populace was angry and frustrated at the lack of progress. Midterm elections, just ended, had gone badly for the Republicans. Congress wanted action as well. The War Department was determined to push ahead with its campaign in Virginia, and by the first week in December, Burnside's 120,000 troops, led by Sumner, Franklin and Hooker, had advanced toward Fredericksburg and formed battle lines on the northeast side of the Rappahannock River. Lee, with Jackson and Longstreet, was dug in on high ground above the town on the southwest side. On December 9, the 12th Corps was ordered into position near Fredericksburg to be in reserve of the main force and ready to support it.

Gordon himself had been feeling ill for some weeks and was unable to go with them. He was showing signs of typhoid fever, so he stayed behind, resting in the Washington area—perhaps Alexandria—near the army's headquarters there. Meanwhile, the 12th Corps, now under a new commander, Major General Henry Slocum, took up a position behind the front lines. The battle there, which took place on December 13, was similar in many respects to Antietam. Lee, Jackson and Longstreet were outnumbered almost two to one, but by virtue of a superior defensive position and better tactics, they fought a much larger force to a standoff, which amounted to another defeat for the Union. The casualty figures, like at Antietam, were staggering. Gordon's men remained in reserve throughout and suffered no casualties. When it was over, Burnside withdrew his forces back across the Rappahannock. Morale in the army took another plunge. Both sides had had enough of winter warfare and settled into quarters. The 12th Corps encamped nearby at the little town of Stafford Court House and remained there from the end of January to mid-April.

Unable to regain his health, Gordon applied for sick leave and, on February 28, left for home, where he remained for the better part of two

months. Little is known of his activities during that time. It is fair to assume that his mother and cousin Lizzie nursed him. Perhaps it was at this time that he began to take notice of the beautiful young woman his little cousin had become; perhaps he even began to see her in a romantic light. He was now almost forty and still single. The horrors of war may have moved him to think of his own mortality and created a desire to marry and start a family. Or perhaps the strong-willed mother just decided that Lizzie was the right one for him and began dropping hints! Whatever the source, an attraction was growing between them.

Gordon, now a brigadier general, late 1862. Looking tired and thin, he shows the effects of months in the field of combat. *Courtesy of the Framingham History Center.*

During Gordon's recuperation, there were developments elsewhere in Massachusetts that would affect his 2nd Massachusetts Infantry. For many months leading up to this time, Governor Andrew had been urging Lincoln to utilize freed blacks in the military. Reluctant to do so at first, Lincoln finally agreed, in part because it was becoming so difficult to find enough able-bodied men to fill the ranks. In January 1863, he gave his approval, and Andrew embarked on the task of raising the first all-black volunteer regiment. It proved impossible to find sufficient numbers of blacks within Massachusetts, so it was necessary to recruit others from throughout the Northern states to meet the quota for a full regiment. The unit was to be commanded by white officers, and Andrew wanted the best available for this difficult task. He called on one of Gordon's young officers, Captain Robert Gould Shaw, to be its commander. Thus, the 54th Massachusetts Volunteer Infantry Regiment was born. Its story has been chronicled in books, as well as a popular motion picture, *Glory*. Shaw and his men would meet their destiny a few months later in an ill-fated assault on Fort Wagner, near Charleston Harbor.

After several weeks, Gordon's health began to improve, and at the end of April, he returned to active duty.

Meanwhile, a large Union force, including the 12th Corps, still stood outside Fredericksburg. Having botched the first battle there, Burnside offered to resign his position. Lincoln quickly accepted and put Major General Joseph Hooker in charge. Anxious to prove himself, Hooker determined to have another go at Lee, and on May 1, he launched another attack. The focus of the fighting was a little removed from Fredericksburg and became known as the Battle of Chancellorsville. It was here where Lee lost one of his most effective generals: "Stonewall" Jackson was wounded and died of complications a few weeks later. Gordon's 2nd Massachusetts Regiment was in the thick of this battle and suffered many dead and wounded. However, Gordon was not with them. Brigadier General Thomas Ruger, another West Pointer who had previously commanded a regiment in Gordon's brigade, was now in command.

On the first day of fighting at Chancellorsville, Gordon was reporting for duty at Fort Monroe in eastern Virginia near Norfolk. He had unsuccessfully requested a return to the command of his old brigade. Here his commanding officer would be General John A. Dix. This was the same location from which McClellan had launched his ill-fated Peninsula Campaign a year earlier. While that action had ended in failure, much of the area around Norfolk remained in Union hands, and Confederate forces led by Longstreet were operating in the area as well. Occupied by Union forces, the city of Suffolk was under threat from Longstreet, so Dix gave Gordon a small division of about four thousand men and sent him to help in the defense of that city, reporting to General John Peck. Like other officers, Gordon traveled in relative comfort:

> [After] *a few preliminaries for my departure were dispatched, with my military family and full equipment of horses and servants, I entered the special train of one passenger and one baggage car that steamed off for Suffolk.*[64]

At Suffolk, Gordon encountered for the first time the "freed slave" problem. The Emancipation Proclamation had taken effect in January, and since then Union lines had been inundated with wandering bands of slaves. General Peck had provided for them within the city bounds. Gordon described what he saw:

> *General Peck deserves great credit for his foresight...He had established a camp for negroes, called the Contraband Camp which I visited...I found a collection of negroes, males and females, of all sizes and colors, packed in houses of their own construction, the whole bearing some resemblance to a village of hottentots. Pine clapboards formed the walls, roofs and doors of the houses which were about six feet long by five feet wide, and six feet high. The front of each and the streets were ornamented with rows of young pines, and in the middle of the village was a square, in which negroes were running, skipping and playing with light hearts.*[65]

Gordon's duties at Suffolk had barely begun when he was ordered back to Norfolk. He and his division were immediately sent far up the York River to a strategic outpost in the little town of West Point,[66] less than fifty miles from Richmond. In the weeks that followed, Gordon and his forces explored the surrounding area, fought skirmishes with Rebels and reconnoitered to within five miles of Richmond. Eventually, it was decided that this outpost was so isolated as to be almost impossible to defend should there be a counterattack, and on May 30, Gordon and his men boarded steamers and abandoned the outpost. Following that, they were engaged in several short-term assignments at different locations on the peninsula, including Yorktown and Williamsburg. He found that he had to deal with the same problem that General Peck was facing. Every day, small bands of slaves would cross the lines into his camp looking for asylum. He did what he could for them, employing some of the able-bodied men in building defenses and some of the women as cooks, laundry ladies and so on. Others of these blacks proved to be quite valuable as scouts. Their knowledge of the local territory meant that they could move about easily to gather information on the strength and movements of the enemy. At this time, a piece of good fortune befell Gordon when his young cousin and former adjutant, Captain Scott, obtained a transfer and rejoined him.

Meanwhile, Lee and his army were not idle. They were on the move once more, this time headed back north to threaten Pennsylvania. The possibility that Lee had taken most of his troops from around Richmond meant that Dix's army, including Gordon's division, might be able to launch a successful attack there. Dix requested additional troops and moved slowly toward Richmond. By the last week in June, he had amassed a force of about twenty thousand and was just a few miles outside the city. After further consultations with Washington, it was decided not to attack but rather to stay in place and keep the pressure on. Therefore, they missed the great battle at Gettysburg. On July 4, they received the welcome news of a hard-fought victory at Gettysburg. Gordon's old regiment had served valiantly in that battle—without him.

When two days passed with no orders from Washington, General Dix, on his own, decided to send some of his troops to help out. He chose Gordon's division for this assignment. On the eighth, they marched to Yorktown, where they boarded steamers that would take them across the river to Baltimore. Here they boarded trains to take them north. At Washington, they stopped long enough for Gordon to have a quick conference with General Halleck, the commander of all forces, and to receive further orders. He was to take his division through Frederick, Maryland, and on to Gettysburg to link up with Meade in the pursuit of Lee. One can hardly imagine the problems involved in moving four thousand men, their supplies and equipment and horses and wagons such a distance. It required twenty-eight cars to carry them all! On the fourteenth, after six days' travel by steamer, by train and on foot, they reached Meade's headquarters near Hagerstown, Maryland. Gordon sought out the general, introduced himself and informed him that he had brought his division of four thousand infantry to assist in defeating Lee. Meade welcomed him cordially. The conversation follows:[67]

Meade: Glad to see you, Sir. Take a seat on the camp-bed, there is no other.

Gordon: I have brought you, Sir, from White House, Virginia, my division of about four thousand infantry. I have travelled with great dispatch, having left there on the eighth, which makes but six days in transferring this command to you, ready to take the field, and of those six, four were marching days.

Meade: You would have done me more good by remaining near Richmond. The whole Rebel army crossed the Potomac this morning.

Gordon: Indeed! (with surprise) We did not remain at Richmond because General Halleck ordered all those troops to be sent to you; and mine have come in hot haste.

Meade: We held a council yesterday, and all my commanders were in favor of not attacking the enemy. I was in favor of doing so, but I did not feel like moving against the advice of my commanders, for they do all the work. But I should have moved this morning at any rate.

One can only image Gordon's feelings at this moment!

Gettysburg proved to be the largest battle of the war so far, involving about 160,000 men, with terrible losses on both sides. The dead and wounded totaled about 51,000. But it was a clear victory for the North. Lee had been stopped and by now was back across the Potomac—with great losses. However, the consensus was that Meade had missed another great opportunity to deal a fatal blow to Lee and his army by failing to carry the battle to him as he tried to flee. Not until the sixteenth of July did he resume.

In developing plans to renew the fight, Meade merged two divisions and put them under Gordon's command, designating it the 1st Division, 11th Corps. As they prepared to carry on, Gordon probably stood on the shores of the Potomac and pondered over the fact that this was the third time, at the same place in two years, that he would cross into Virginia. The next few weeks were spent in a futile effort to find and destroy Lee's and Longstreet's armies. Then, on August 5, Gordon received urgent orders to report with his full division to General Halleck at Alexandria for a new assignment.

Chapter 10

THE SIEGE OF CHARLESTON AND
CAPTURE OF FORT WAGNER,
SUMMER/FALL OF 1863

Just a few days later, on August 15, Gordon and his full division were landing on a little strip of sand called Folly Island, near the mouth of Charleston Harbor in South Carolina. They had been transferred here by the War Department to take part in the siege of that city. In recent days, the prospects for victory by the Union appeared much improved. Until a few weeks ago, the war had felt like a stalemate, but in early July, Union forces achieved two major victories: one in the east at Gettysburg and a second in the west at Vicksburg on the Mississippi. The latter split the Confederacy in two and left that river, with its vital supply routes, under Union control. At last there was reason for optimism in the North.

Most Northerners felt that the city of Charleston deserved to receive the harshest treatment. South Carolina had been the leader of the rebellion—the first to secede—and Rebel militia at Charleston had fired the first shots when it bombarded Fort Sumter. Its capture would be of great symbolic, if not strategic, significance. In a letter to his mother, Gordon had expressed the prevailing feeling: "I would like to see Charleston bombarded & destroyed."[68] The South was equally protective of it. In fact, President Davis had said that it must be defended at all costs. The defense of the city and port was in the hands of Confederate general Pierre Beauregard from Louisiana, but he had only a small force of about six thousand men under his command.

Early on in the war, the Union navy had set up blockades around the major Southern ports, Charleston among them. Its objectives were twofold: 1) to cut

An encampment of Union troops on the shores of Morris Island, 1863. Ships in the background are part of the blockade and siege of the harbor and city of Charleston, South Carolina. *Courtesy of Library of Congress, LC-DIG-04745.*

off all overseas commerce, especially trade in weapons and munitions, and 2) to prevent the exportation of cotton. The cotton trade was vital to the Southern economy. Without access to its foreign markets, the South could not survive.

The navy shared the country's desire to punish Charleston. Already in position there, it began to develop a plan to capture the city. The War Department agreed and gave its approval. It planned to employ its most powerful weapons, ironclads, monitors and heavily armed sailing ships to bombard the city into submission, but first they would have to get into the well-defended harbor. Entrance to the harbor was through a narrow channel running between two low-lying barrier islands (Morris and Sullivan's). Equipped with heavy artillery, Confederate forts were positioned on both to guard the harbor mouth. Fort Sumter sat just inside on a little island. Along the shores of the harbor were numerous artillery installations as well.

The naval strategists reasoned that a combined land and sea assault would be required to overcome these obstacles, so they enlisted the aid of the army. The plan depended on extensive use of land-based heavy artillery, so Army General Quincy A. Gillmore, an expert in this type of weaponry, was assigned to lead the land forces. Naval operations were under the direction of Rear Admiral Dahlgren. The land phase of the plan began on July 10 when a Union force of more than eleven thousand men, with ninety-eight artillery pieces, went ashore on the southern tip of Morris Island. Their first objective was to destroy Fort Wagner. Once that was achieved, Gillmore would set up his heavy artillery and undertake the destruction of Sumter. Morris Island was little more than a sandbar, roughly one mile wide and four miles long, and the fort lay about midway.

Hoping to catch the Confederates by surprise, Gillmore launched a quick frontal assault the day after landing, July 11. But the Confederates were there, ready for him. His force was repelled with heavy losses. Taking a more cautious approach in the days that followed, he advanced his troops to within half a mile of the fort and then laid siege to it. At the same time, he set up his artillery and began hammering away. Naval vessels lying just off shore joined in. On the eighteenth, he ordered a second assault—another charge across open sands along the shoreline. This time the assault was led by the 54th Massachusetts, the all-black unit created by Governor Andrew and led by young Colonel Robert Shaw, who had trained with Gordon. The results were even worse than before. Shaw and several other officers were killed, as were hundreds of their men. Shaw's body was dumped into a mass grave together with those of his fallen black troops.[69]

Morris Island, headquarters of the field officer of the trenches, August 1863. In the assault on Fort Wagner, Gordon's forces had to trench their way across open ground (beach and sand dunes) in order to avoid the fire of the Confederates. *Courtesy of the Library of Congress, LC-DIG-cwp-04728.*

Shortly after this episode, Gillmore asked for an additional eight thousand ground forces.[70] It was then that Gordon received urgent orders to report, with his division, to General Halleck in Alexandria. Upon their arrival a few days later, they learned that they were to be the reinforcements that Gillmore had requested. On August 11, Gordon and his six thousand men boarded steamships at Newport News, Virginia, and four days later they landed a few hundred yards from the southern tip of Morris Island. It is not known whether Gordon knew at the time about the very recent fate of his young officer, Colonel Shaw, and the 54th Massachusetts, on this very island. He set up his encampment on Folly Island, adjacent to Morris, and reported to Gillmore to begin preparations for a new assault on Wagner.

Through the rest of July and into August, Gillmore contented himself with shelling the fort, while Gordon and his men moved ever closer by a

The Swamp Angel, Morris Island, 1863. From a location near Fort Wagner, Union soldiers set up this battery, which they nicknamed the "Swamp Angel." This and other heavy artillery bombarded Fort Sumter and even the city of Charleston for months. *Courtesy of the Library of Congress, LC-USZ62-50303.*

series of diagonal trenches in the sand. The navy cooperated by bombarding the fort constantly from the sea as well. It took several weeks for Gillmore to get his largest artillery pieces in position and functioning. His most powerful weapon, a three-hundred-pound Parrot cannon, was nicknamed "Swamp Angel" by the men.

On the seventeenth, Swamp Angel was ready. Rather than waiting until Fort Wagner had been taken, Gillmore began the bombardment of Sumter. He predicted that it would be reduced to a pile of rubble in twelve days and that the navy would be able to pass unopposed into the harbor. This prediction would prove to be completely wrong. Gordon's land forces focused their efforts on preparations to take Fort Wagner, trenching closer and closer each day and throwing up works to protect the big artillery pieces. At the same time, Gillmore began to fire a few shells into the city of Charleston itself. He sent a letter to Beauregard demanding that he surrender the city. Beauregard replied that the shelling of civilians was "an act of inexcusable barbarity"[71] and ignored the demands. By September 1, the ground forces had advanced to within two hundred yards of Fort Wagner.

The time for the planned assault on Wagner was fast approaching when, during the night of September 6, the Confederate forces abandoned it and evacuated all troops from the fort and island. Gillmore declared that he had achieved his goal. Not only was all of Morris Island in his hands, but Sumter appeared to be little more than a rubble pile as well, so he assumed that the Confederates had evacuated it. Almost immediately, the navy moved in to occupy it. They landed a force of several hundred sailors and marines under cover of darkness, only to discover that there was still a sizable force defending it. The results were disastrous. Their assault was repulsed, with several killed and many captured. Relations between Gillmore and Dahlgren had been strained from the start, but this event caused a complete breakdown. The idea of a combined sea and land campaign made sense on paper, but in practice it worked poorly. The two services argued about tactics and command. Each blamed the other for the lack of progress.

Gordon and his troops settled into a routine existence. Life on Folly Island was a study in contrasts. Gordon marveled at the beauty of the place on the one hand:

> *Very tropical is this long and narrow bit of land. With a sand heap for its eastern, and a marsh for its western boundary, while between was vegetable*

life rank and luxurious. The palmetto reaches its cabbage head and its long, sword-like leaf upward toward the gorgeous magnolia; the southern pines like stately sentinels stand erect in the forest; parasitical mosses droop from the trees, and creeping vines cover the earth.[72]

At the same time, it presented a most difficult locale for the encampment of six thousand men:

Here, too, crowded upon the sand-hills, to escape the marsh, seeking the seabreeze to kill the malaria,—here were the camps, and cook persons, and properties of my command…The population was too crowded to allow each man a house and a bit of land. One A tent will hold three men if they lie close and don't kick around much; sometimes we put in four; the area of four was just equal to the superficial area of the tent. One could not stand straight for the eaves came down to the ground. A company of sixty men lived in fifteen such tents—seven in one row, and eight opposite; and between was what we called a street, varying in width according to the room for the encampment…At one end of this spacious avenue were the officer's tents, also in a row; at the other was the kitchen, while just beyond were other company tents, miserable imitations of civilized life.

As Gordon said, here was the equivalent of a small New England town, positioned on a piece of land the size of a single cow pasture. There was no good water anywhere on the island, and sanitation was extremely difficult. He reported that in one brigade, where conditions were unusually crowded, almost one-third of his force was sick at any time, with dysentery being the primary problem. The bombardment of Sumter continued through the fall and into the winter.

One of Gordon's responsibilities was to set up a defensive perimeter around their position and maintain outposts to monitor enemy movements. The area on the inland side of Folly and Morris Islands was a jigsaw puzzle of small islands, separated by inlets, streams and marshes, the major inlet being known as Stono River. To surveil these locales and maintain skirmish lines and outposts here, Gordon had at his disposal a small gunboat, the *Pawnee*, skippered by a Captain Balch. In the months that followed, they became close friends as they plied the waters together to maintain a defensive perimeter. More than once they stumbled on enemy batteries concealed along riverbanks and came under fire, and they constantly had to watch for floating mines, or "torpedoes" as they called them.

A kind of uneasy truce existed between Gordon's troops and the Confederates. They often talked to one another across the narrow inlets and streams that separated them. They swapped rumors about what was going on in other theaters of operations, exchanged newspapers from their respective sources and tried to glean bits of information about one another's troop movements. There was an occasional skirmish, but nothing of any import.

Some of the brigadiers under Gordon were of German immigrant stock. One, General Schimmelfening, had been an officer in the service of one of the German states, and Gordon enjoyed long conversations with him. Many of the troops in Schimmelfening's brigade were German as well. For Gordon, the sense of closeness that he had with his old brigade was missing now because he did not have the personal investment. However, he soldiered on, always giving 100 percent to whatever task he was assigned. He had also learned that General Gillmore was a man quite full of himself who often boasted of his successes, real and imagined. He was quick to blame others for his failures and shortcomings, which was just the sort of behavior that Gordon abhorred.

In early October, Gordon was granted a leave. Departing Hilton Head Island by steamer on October 10, he landed in New York on the thirteenth. After attending to some business there, he traveled home to Framingham, arriving on November 1.[73] Some rest, home cooking, the company of loved ones and seeing Lizzie again were tonics for the war-weary soldier. By now, he and Lizzie were talking of marriage. It gave him a lift, for he had been feeling discouraged about his prospects in the war. When he got back to Folly Island on November 1, he was feeling somewhat depressed. The rumors that Gillmore was under consideration for promotion to major general may have been a factor in his mood. But he found his way back to the job at hand. In his words, "I went resolutely to my work, shut out thought and memory, and in the living present found content."[74]

The year 1863 came to a close with the Confederates still entrenched in Fort Sumter. By January of '64, after months of continuous bombardment, the fort's exterior was little more than a rubble heap, but somehow parts of the interior, the so-called bomb-proofs, were intact, as were a few of the gun emplacements, and the Stars and Bars still flew from an improvised flagpole. The shelling continued at a much reduced rate. Weary of the failed attempts, the War Department decided to refocus its efforts in this theater. Florida would become the next objective. Charleston Harbor remained blockaded, but the city itself had not been taken. Gordon summed up: "The bombardment of Charleston was of no service in bringing about peace, but it satisfied a certain thirst for vengeance."[75]

During this time, the only blemish on Gordon's otherwise spotless military record occurred. In retrospect, it was a silly affair that probably grew out of a clash of egos. As operations at Charleston Harbor wound down, specifically on January 15, 1864, Gordon received an order to transfer the 40th Massachusetts from his command to Gillmore's on Hilton Head Island. He carried out the order the next day. About fifteen men and two or three officers from this unit were overlooked somehow and did not go along with their regiment, instead being left behind. Gordon later claimed that they were on a special assignment and that he simply was not aware of them. In any case, Gillmore found out about this and sent Gordon an angry communication that demanded an explanation. Instead of replying in a respectful way, Gordon wrote a nasty letter in response, suggesting that Gillmore had disrespected him. Very upset by this, Gillmore had Gordon arrested and charged with disobeying orders, neglect of duty and insubordination. For this minor offense he was tried in a court-martial by a jury of his fellow officers. He was acquitted of the charges of disobedience to orders and neglect of duty, but he was found guilty of insubordination because of the letter he had sent to Gillmore.[76] Like all courts-martial, the verdict was subject to review by the War Department, and the conviction was probably vacated at a later date, although proof of this is yet to be found.

By the end of 1863, Union forces were on the move on several fronts, and the momentum was on their side. President Lincoln, anxious to bring things to a swift end, issued a proclamation in December intended to make it easier for Southern states to be reunited with the Union. It was called the Proclamation of Amnesty and Reconstruction. Under its provisions, if 10 percent of the registered voters (based on the 1860 election) took an oath of allegiance to the Union and agreed to abide by the emancipation law, they could rejoin the Union, call a state convention and write a new state constitution, which must include a clause outlawing slavery. In return, citizens' property rights would be restored. It was dubbed the "Ten Percent Plan." Many Northerners felt that the proclamation was much too lenient, but Lincoln pushed on with it. During 1864, Louisiana and Tennessee would take advantage of the new rule. Washington set its sights on Florida as another state that potentially might be brought in under this policy.

Chapter 11
A Futile Episode in Florida and on to the Deep South, Spring/Summer of 1864

While Gordon was toiling on the barrier islands of South Carolina, Union forces elsewhere were making significant gains. Grant and Sherman, after a protracted struggle in Tennessee and northern Georgia, had achieved major victories at Chattanooga. As 1864 began, hopes of success were growing in the North. Grant had so impressed Lincoln that the president brought him to Virginia to command all Union forces.

In 1861, Florida's legislature had been quick to vote for secession, even though public opinion in that state was by no means unanimous. Many citizens had reservations about taking that step. Support had been fairly strong during the early days of the war, but by this time it was much weaker. Union forces occupied a large strip of coast in the Jacksonville area. Nevertheless, there was still some support for the Confederate cause, and even a few small units of militia operated here and there. Much of the state was a no-man's land with little civil authority; whole districts had fallen under the control of Union loyalists. This was especially so along the eastern coast in the Jacksonville area.

In Washington, leaders of the Republican party saw an opportunity not only for the Union but for their party as well. They had their eyes on the fall elections. They hoped that a series of small, fast-moving attacks at key points around that state would result in its surrender. Their plan was to have Union loyalists installed in major offices and have them adopt the terms of Lincoln's amnesty program. This would make them eligible to vote in the fall—Republican, of course. Lincoln himself became interested in the idea and, after some deliberations, gave it his blessing. To General Gillmore he wrote:[77]

EXECUTIVE MANSION
Washington, January 13, 1864

Major General Gillmore, I understand an effort is being made by some worthy gentlemen to reconstruct a loyal State government in Florida. Florida is in your department, and it is not unlikely that you may be there in person. I have given Mr Hay[78] *a commission of major, and sent him to you with some blank books and other blanks to aid in the reconstruction. He will explain as to the manner of using the blanks and also my general views on the subject. It is desirable for all to cooperate, but if irreconcilable differences of opinion shall arise, you are master. I wish the thing to be done in the most speedy way possible, so that when done it will be within the range of the late proclamation on the subject.*[79] *The detail labor, of course, will have to be done by others, but I shall be greatly obliged if you will give it such general supervision as you can find convenient with your more strictly military duties.*

Yours very truly,
Abraham Lincoln

Gillmore put Brigadier General Truman Seymour in charge of the operation, and with a force of about five thousand, he pushed inland from Jacksonville on February 9. Their objective was a rail junction at Lake City. Control of this strategic junction would cut the state off from its Confederate neighbors. The operation went smoothly for the first few days. On the fifteenth, Gillmore, absent from the field of action and lacking information, communicated to Washington that the state had been "liberated." There was just one problem—he forgot to tell the Confederates. Unbeknownst to him and Seymour, they had received advance information of the plan and had sent troops from neighboring Georgia to Lake City to reinforce the small local force. At the little town of Olustee near Lake City, Union forces stumbled into a trap and were badly beaten. It was not a big battle, but the percentage of casualties on the Union side was unusually high. One of the

Union regiments involved in this action was the all-black 54th Massachusetts. Seymour and his men straggled back into Jacksonville a few days later.

Meanwhile, Gordon and his division were winding up their activities on the Charleston Harbor islands. On March 7, they vacated their strongholds there and moved to an encampment on Hilton Head Island, where they spent several weeks resting and preparing for the next campaign. Gordon hoped to be assigned once again to the Army of the Potomac,[80] but that was not to be. On May 1, he and his men received orders to report to Jacksonville, Florida, where Gordon was to take command of all Union forces. It was to be a temporary assignment, filling in for General William Birney. Despite the defeat at Olustee, the amnesty plan was going forward in the Jacksonville area, and Gordon was expected to continue its implementation. When he took command on May 7, however, his first priority was to familiarize himself with the many Union outposts, which were small groups of soldiers strung out along the eastern shore of the St. John's River. A week later, he mounted his trusted horse, Ashby, and away they went. It took them just five hours to cover the forty-one miles to St. Augustine. What a magnificent animal! The next morning, he continued on to Picolata, visiting each outpost of his new command along the way. Back at Jacksonville a few days later, he applied himself to reconstruction:

> *Loyal Floridians flocked to my headquarters…My time was taken up with…reviews of troops, conferences with the provost-marshal, devising new and better police and sanitary measures; with organization of a court for civil administration; with oaths of allegiance; with calling a convention to send delegates to the National Conference[81] for a Presidential Nomination…with revising a printed memorial from citizens to the President asking protection and permanent occupation of the State.[82]*

After three weeks, however, this work was cut short by hostile activities on the southern reaches of the St. John's. Confederate forces had crossed to the east side of the river near Welaka and were on the offensive. Gordon learned where their base was located, assembled what troops he could and took off in pursuit. He arrived at their encampment to find that they had fled. After destroying all they could find, he and his men returned to Jacksonville. On June 2, General Birney resumed his command, and Gordon was ordered to report to the adjutant general in Washington. He had been attached to the

Department of the South for just short of a year. The effort to bring Florida back into the Union in time for the 1864 election eventually failed, and it remained a Confederate state until the end of the war.

Gordon was full of hope that he would be rejoining the Army of the Potomac, but upon his arrival in Washington, he learned that he had been assigned to duty in the Deep South, where he was to take command of a division in General Edward Canby's Army of West Mississippi. Canby's forces operated along the Gulf of Mexico and up the Mississippi River as far as north as Memphis. Deeply disappointed and unsure of what the future might hold, Gordon requested a few days' leave and rushed home to Framingham. There he and Lizzie were united in marriage in a simple ceremony at the family home.[83] Reverend Samuel Robbins of the First Parish officiated. On June 16, Gordon was on a steamship, this time bound for New Orleans. Ten days later, as he approached that city, a moment of nostalgia gripped him as he described the scene:

> *Neither waste nor desolation had touched the plantations and cultivated fields on the Lower Mississippi, though most of the Rebel owners had fled from their stately homes. Near the city the New Orleans barracks came into view… Eighteen years had passed since, on my way to Mexico with General Scott, I had drilled my company of Mounted Riflemen upon that field, lived in those barracks, and galloped with my companions to the St. Charles Hotel.*[84]

He soon discovered that Lincoln's amnesty program was in full swing here. Although parts of this state were still under Confederate control, the city itself had been in Union hands since April 1862, when Admiral David Farragut had executed a brilliant takeover of the city when he brought a fleet of heavily armed vessels up the Mississippi. Since then, it had operated under a Union military governorship. By now, many of its citizens had taken the oath of allegiance, and a convention was in session to draft a new state constitution that would outlaw slavery. The lifeblood of this city was its commerce and trade, and as a practical matter, the people and political leaders just decided to accept the reality of their situation and move on. The presence of Union soldiers was tolerated.

Canby planned for Gordon to take command of one of his divisions, a force numbering about five thousand based almost five hundred miles up the Mississippi at Memphis. They were supposed to have orders to move down the Mississippi to a location near Natchez. Gordon was instructed to rendezvous with them, take command and bring them to their destination. However, Canby also had forces occupying the city of Little Rock, and they were at risk. Confederate forces were still threatening the city with sporadic attacks. If they should need reinforcements, Gordon was instructed to take his division up the White River into Arkansas and set up a base there—a rather complicated situation!

Gordon departed New Orleans by river steamer on July 2 expecting to meet up with his new command in a few days, but they were nowhere to be found. This began what he later described as a "shuttlecock existence." In search of his division, he went all the way to Memphis, where the commanding officer declared that he had no troops available. This news triggered a series of trips between Memphis and points south, dealing with constantly changing and conflicting orders and with general confusion as to the mission. Eventually, he and a small force of 1,500 men and some artillery met at the mouth of the White River. He cobbled together what he could in the way of supplies and transportation and headed into Arkansas on the White River. After several weeks and a few minor skirmishes, he found himself and his little band en route to Louisiana for reassignment.

In each of these moves, of course, he was accompanied by his retinue of staff, servants, horses and baggage. During his travels along the lower Mississippi, he became aware of a vast illicit trade in cotton.[85] The textile mills of the North desperately needed cotton. Washington tried a number of different plans to allow some controlled trade. Finally, Lincoln put the problem in the hands of the Treasury Department, which developed a system of licensing trustworthy individuals to purchase Southern cotton at government-regulated prices for resale to the Northern mills. Also, any cotton captured by the military was to be sold at auction under treasury supervision, with the proceeds going to the government. Inevitably, a black market developed, and in many cases military personnel—from both sides— were involved. The temptation for men in high command to profit by turning a blind eye to such activities for a fee was great, and many succumbed. It was rumored that General Benjamin Butler, during his time as the military governor of New Orleans, had become quite rich engaging in such practices. As one would expect, Gordon was appalled by such behavior.

He was called back to New Orleans in early August, when the district developed a new hot spot: Mobile Bay, Alabama. Before the war, Mobile had been the chief U.S. port for the shipment of cotton around the world. But since early in the war, a naval blockade had all but shut it down. Now, however, it appeared that the Confederates might attempt to reopen it by force. There was a navy yard in the bay with shipbuilding facilities, where they had recently finished construction on a massive new ironclad. Union military strategists decided that it was time to go in, eliminate this threat and take the city. Gordon was informed that he would have a part in this operation.

The geography of the area bore a striking resemblance to that of Charleston, South Carolina. There was a harbor and a large city. In both places, there was a single good channel leading into the harbor, which was protected by forts positioned on barrier islands to either side. But there were differences, too. Charleston Harbor was perhaps two or three miles at its widest point, small enough so that shore batteries could blanket its entire area. Control there would require capture of the city and the surrounding area. By contrast, Mobile Bay was very large—almost thirty miles long and, in places, more than ten miles wide. Once inside, ships could operate safely out of range of any shore batteries, but first they would have to run the gauntlet at the entrance to the bay. The bay could then be controlled.

On August 5, Admiral David Farragut, with a flotilla of Union ships including ironclads, successfully blasted his way into Mobile Bay. The story of this exploit was broadcast in tabloids throughout the North, and his famous cry, "Damn the torpedoes, full speed ahead,"[86] became legend. Whether he actually said that is open to conjecture, but witnesses confirmed that he did take a position high up in the rigging of his wooden warship, the *Hartford*, and directed the ships and guns of his fleet as they sailed into the channel, past the enemy forts and into the bay. Once inside, they sank the new Confederate ironclad, *Tennessee*, as well as many smaller Confederate warships, and anchored safely out of reach of the forts and other shore batteries. This achievement, coupled with his capture of New Orleans two years earlier, turned him into one of the great "folk heroes" of the war.

Like the assault on Charleston, this was a combined land and sea assault, and Gordon commanded a portion of the land forces. His immediate superior was General Gordon Granger. Their first objectives were the two forts at the bay entrance. Gordon and his men landed to the west and quickly occupied Fort Gaines, which they found had been abandoned a day earlier. Granger and his men surrounded the other, and a bombardment from land and sea

A graphic depiction of the Battle of Mobile Bay, August 5, 1864, when Farragut and the Union navy broke through. Gordon and his forces went ashore near here and seized Fort Gaines, which they found had been abandoned by the Confederates a day earlier. *Courtesy of the Library of Congress, LC-USZ—49465.*

began. In less than two days, a white flag of surrender was hoisted, and six hundred men and officers marched out into the hands of their Union captors. The will of the South to carry on the fight was showing signs of weakening.

One day, Admiral Farragut invited Gordon to dine aboard his ship. They spent a cordial evening together and found that they enjoyed each other's company. As the evening wore on, Farragut amused Gordon with yarns about his life in the navy dating from the War of 1812 to the present. In the weeks that followed, they spent many an evening together. These good friends would soon meet again in Virginia.

Disease was always a threat in the overcrowded military encampments of the day. Maintaining good sanitation was difficult. Here in the South, too, mosquito-borne diseases such as yellow fever and malaria were a constant problem. "Sickness was on the increase; malarial fever patients filled our temporary hospitals," Gordon wrote. So when he began to feel ill, it was no surprise. His symptoms started with a slight fever and then progressed to chills and headache—telltale signs of malaria. Despite his condition, he carried on with his duties.

Toward the end of August, General Granger was called to New Orleans and left Gordon in command of all the ground forces there. On the twenty-fifth, the plan to attack Mobile was put into action when a force of about two thousand infantry, accompanied by artillery, landed on the mainland at Cedar Point. They moved inland and along the west shore of the bay toward the city. In the midst of this operation, Gordon's illness worsened:

> *Absolute prostration and utter helplessness oppressed me for the first time in my life. The heat in the bay was not relieved by the wind which our boat had stirred. A sudden chill in all this heat, an unbearable suffocation, followed by a burning fever, sent me to the shore, whence I was carried to my camp bed, and there restored to life.*[87]

After dosing himself with quinine, he was able to travel to New Orleans, where he was immediately granted twenty days' sick leave beginning on September 7. He also received permission to make application for a transfer of duty to the north. Although he had no way of knowing at the time, this was to be his farewell to battlefield warfare; the future would take him in an entirely different direction. Major General Canby determined that his forces were spread too thin and opted not to proceed further with the land attack. The navy remained in the bay and kept the port closed. A token land force was left to keep the forts and entrance to the bay under Union control, and by the spring of 1865, Canby's forces had advanced deep into Alabama. The city finally fell in April.

Chapter 12

WITH GENERALS GRANT AND BUTLER IN EASTERN VIRGINIA, FALL/WINTER OF 1864–1865

While Gordon had been on duty in the Deep South, the pace of Union successes in other theaters was quickening. Through the summer, General William T. Sherman had rolled up victory upon victory in the Southern heartland, culminating in the capture of Atlanta on September 2. Gordon's old regiment, the 2nd Massachusetts, had joined Sherman's Army of the Tennessee earlier and was photographed encamped on the lawn in front of Atlanta City Hall. Lincoln had brought Grant to Virginia in the spring of 1864 to take command of all Union forces, hoping that he would accomplish what none of his previous generals had done: the defeat of Robert E. Lee and the Army of Northern Virginia. Grant had designed a strategy and put it into action in May, but he found Lee to be a formidable opponent.

After some initial small successes, Grant's drive bogged down. By the beginning of fall, the two armies were entrenched along a line extending roughly from Richmond to Petersburg and fighting a battle of attrition. Grant's forces consisted of the Army of the Potomac, commanded by Meade and himself, and the Army of the James, under Major General Benjamin Butler. Lee's Army of Northern Virginia was supplemented by a sizable force commanded by Beauregard, but they were badly outnumbered and running low on food, ammunition and other supplies. Grant, on the other hand, was headquartered at a spot called City Point on the James River, where there was an enormous Union supply depot. The Union had all the supplies it could want.

Lieutenant General Ulysses S. Grant, summer of 1864, after taking command of all Union forces. In the fall, Gordon had recovered sufficiently from malaria to return to active duty. He was assigned to Grant's command. *Courtesy of the Library of Congress, LC-DIG-cwpb-06945.*

After three weeks' convalescence at home, Gordon's malaria had subsided, and on September 27 he reported back for duty at Fort Monroe in Virginia. He was summoned to City Point to meet with Grant. Gordon described their meeting:

> *I arrived at four o'clock in the afternoon. General Grant was near the landing within the square which held his own tent and the tents of his staff. As I approached a mutual recognition followed, though we had not met since we were in the city of Mexico under Scott. Grant was talking to his staff in an easy and familiar way, when General Hunter, who had come up on the steamer, introduced me. "Why," said the General, "Gordon, I knew you a quarter of a century ago." We were together two years at West Point. Cadet Grant graduated in 1844. It was twenty years since I had first met him. "Come to my tent" he added in an easy and cordial way; and we directed our steps towards a good-sized wall-tent, with a carpeted floor and but little camp furniture, pitched on the greensward of a rich estate on the bank of*

the James. The scene, with the flag flying in front, near the cottage of the owner of this domain, surrounded with hedges, shrubbery, and roses, was both beautiful and picturesque. Beyond, where soldiers overran, batteries defaced, and hungry mules destroyed, the usual desolation and destruction were displayed. Grant offered cigars. Of course he was smoking, indeed he was rarely without a cigar. He made the frank admission, however, that he "smoked too much," and thought he "felt better when he hankered after a cigar" than when he "smoked one." The General's mail was handed him. Some letters he read with great interest, one from a mutual friend...Another was from the President, "Uncle Abe," as Grant called him..."I do get a great many letters telling me how to take Richmond"...The conversation lasted for two or three hours and was shared with large numbers of civilians of note and general officers who had dropped in, all of whom however could do little more than listen, for the General held the floor and did most of the talking. Grant is a much better looking man than his photographs represent him to be. I could easily discover the old resolute look I had often noted when he was a grey-coated cadet at West Point; and it gave me every encouragement that at last the right man was in the right place.

I left Grant's headquarters with assurances that I should be ordered on duty with his army. On the 3rd of October I received a dispatch from General Grant at City Point, dated October 1, directing me to report to General Butler. This assignment was not what I had anticipated from the General-in-Chief, but there was no remedy for it, so I prepared to obey, with the belief or hope that it was only a stepping stone to better things beyond.[88]

This seemingly routine decision of Grant's would have long-range consequences for Gordon.

Before the war, Butler had been very active in Massachusetts politics and served in both branches of the legislature. Consequently, he was very well connected. He became a brigadier general in the State Militia, but it was a purely political appointment. He lacked any real military training or experience. Because of Governor Andrew's foresight in readying Massachusetts militias early, when they were called on in April 1861 to go to Baltimore and secure the route to Washington from the north, Butler did an effective job and received much credit for it. Lincoln held him in high regard thereafter and commissioned him a major general of U.S. volunteers. Throughout the war, his record was very mixed. In administrative positions, such as military governorship of New

Orleans, he was effective, although the people of the South hated him. He kept tight control over the city, and it was rumored that he profited greatly through his duties there, earning the nickname "Beast" Butler. Jefferson Davis declared him a criminal and ruled that if he were ever captured, he was to be executed. On the battlefield, however, Butler was quite ineffective and regularly lost battles. He left the post at New Orleans in late 1862 and was put in a similar position as military governor of the District of Eastern Virginia and North Carolina in 1863. Here he again performed well, although years later, Gordon would describe his performance in less than glowing terms:

> *The control of the entire region...was exercised by Butler. He made the laws and administered them, dealt out justice and inflicted punishment, levied fines and collected taxes. An enormous fund, said to amount to an unexpended quarter of a million dollars, was thus created, of which Butler disposed of as he pleased. Under the permissive power of martial law, he conducted and managed every movement of every person within his department.*[89]

Such unlimited power is always a temptation for abuse, but in Butler's case, he apparently thought it was a privilege of rank. The combination of one who would bend the law to his own benefit, and another, Gordon, who had a visceral dislike of such behavior was a recipe for trouble. Eventually, the two would clash.

Earlier in the year, Grant and Butler had been working together. Grant knew of Butler's lackluster record on the battlefield but could not overrule Lincoln's estimation of the man. He wanted to squeeze Lee from two directions, west and east, and Butler, with the Army of the James, composed of thirty-three thousand men, would have to be part of the plan. He was to attack Lee from the east. Landing his forces on the shore of the James River, Butler began an advance toward Petersburg. Through the month of May, they fought numerous small battles, losing most of them. The campaign, later known as the Bermuda One Hundred, was an overall failure. Grant was not pleased.

This was the situation into which Gordon stepped in the fall of 1864. He arrived at Butler's headquarters on October 13 and learned that he was to be given the command of a division in the 10th Corps. He was elated at the prospect of returning to the field of combat, but before he could assume his new duties, the malaria recurred. Desperately ill again, he returned to Fort Monroe, where he received medical treatment and was advised to take another sick leave. He did so, and it began to look like his days as a field commander were over. His health was so unpredictable that perhaps he should no longer subject himself to the rigors of that life, nor should he endanger the lives of men under him by his own fragility.

The presidential election was soon to take place, and there was unrest in the North. People were tired of the war. The number of casualties continued to mount every day, and sentiment for some kind of settlement was growing. George McClellan, now retired, was running against Lincoln on the Democratic ticket. New York City had been the site of antiwar riots the previous year, so Lincoln and his cabinet decided to deploy troops around that city on election day to quell any disturbances. General Butler was given the job. Gordon, still quite ill, was recuperating in a hotel in New York City when he heard of this and contacted Butler to offer assistance. Butler agreed, and in the days just before the election a full division from the Army of the James was transported to a location near the city. Gordon and Butler set up their headquarters in the Hoffman House, one of the city's posh hotels, and together they developed a plan: they would commandeer ferryboats, put troops on board and station them along the shores of Manhattan on the East and Hudson Rivers, out of sight but ready to move in if trouble broke out. They even had light artillery pieces on board. On November 8, election day, voting took place without incident, and Lincoln was reelected. During their time together in this operation, Gordon agreed to be Butler's chief of staff[90] on a temporary basis. For the time being, the two seemed to get along.

Following the election, and still quite ill, Gordon described his movements in the next few days in his diary:[91]

> *Tuesday, Nov. 22, 1864*
> *Leave this day for Framingham to spend Thanksgiving and then return to Fortress Monroe. Arrived this PM at the Hoffman House in N.Y. [illegible] complimentary sent me from Office.*

> *Wednesday, Nov. 23, 1864*
> *At Framingham. Rode all night, and arrived here at 6 A.M. Last evening at Hoffman House, saw poor old Gen'l Scott, dining alone at a small*

table. To the body failing and fainting into the [illegible]. *Poor man, his grandeur is of the past, but the* [illegible] *are still grand in their decay.*

Saturday, Nov. 26, 1864
Arrived tonight at home from Boston, where with mother & wife had grand Thanksgiving.[92] *Found upon my arrival that Butler has sent me an order by telegram to Fortress Monroe and there organize a committee. This as well—all my Drs. agree that I am* [illegible].

The Union's naval blockade of Southern ports had been quite effective, but one remaining port on the Atlantic coast of the Confederacy was open in Wilmington, North Carolina. Situated at the head of a long, narrow bay, it was guarded by Fort Fisher—a situation much like Charleston and Mobile. In December '64, a plan was developed to capture the fort and close the port. Butler was given one more chance to prove himself a capable military leader. With a large force from the Army of the James, he departed Fort Monroe in Virginia on December 13. A fiasco followed. On the night of the twenty-third, Butler led several thousand men ashore. Naval vessels stood offshore bombarding the fort, and their advance went as planned. Officers on the ground felt that they had it within their grasp when, inexplicably, the order to retreat sounded and the attack was abandoned. Butler hastily loaded his troops back onto the ships and returned to Fort Monroe. In his report, he claimed that the enemy had overwhelming force. (Gordon had another view: Years later he would say Butler simply "was frightened away.")[93]

Grant was furious. He made a personal appeal to Lincoln requesting the authority to relieve the man of his command. Under the circumstances, Lincoln had little choice. On January 9, Butler was sent home to Massachusetts to await further orders. He would forever claim that he had been victimized by a cabal of regular army generals, including Grant and Gordon. He still had powerful friends in Washington, and he wasn't going to let this happen without a fight. Through his connections, he was able to obtain a hearing before the Joint Congressional Committee on the Conduct of the War. While he was conducting his own defense, however, General Alfred Terry, with the same force, returned to Cape Fear and captured Fort Fisher in a matter of days. That put an end to Butler's claims. However, Gordon's involvement with Butler was not over:

At this period the War Department was once more aroused by rumors that a large trade in contraband of war was being carried on from and through Norfolk. Grant was ordered to appoint a military commission to examine into this matter and to try suspected persons.[94]

Grant had long heard rumors that Union supplies, such as food, clothing and perhaps even arms, were being traded to the enemy for cotton, which was then resold to Northern mills at a huge profit.

Gordon was the man chosen to undertake this unenviable assignment, perhaps because of his background in law, or more likely because of his reputation as a man of impeccable honesty. On January 21, he assembled the commission in Norfolk and began the investigation. It came to light that one of Butler's subordinates, Brigadier General George F. Shepley, had colluded with him in this illegal trade. Shepley had been with Butler in New Orleans, so they were not newcomers to such activities. It was also found that Butler's brother-in-law, Fisher Hildreth from Lowell, was a player, too. These individuals were directly responsible for "supplies from the Department of Virginia and North Carolina" being "poured directly into the departments of the Rebel Commissary and Quartermaster,"[95] making them all quite rich. The hearing lasted a month, and in the midst of it, Shepley was relieved of his command. Gordon was appointed to take his place as military and civil governor of the District of Eastern Virginia. After deposing fifty witnesses, the commission produced a scathing sixty-page report denouncing Butler and his cohorts. As a result, several of Butler's associates were temporarily imprisoned. Butler was very bitter about these events, and relations between him and Gordon soured.

Captain Henry Scott had remained with Gordon as his adjutant since the spring of 1863, but the time had come for him to make a change. In January 1865, he joined the 4th Massachusetts Cavalry with a rank of major. In the coming months, it was part of the Army of the James, under Major General Edward Ord, and took part in the Appomattox Campaign, which culminated in Lee's capitulation. Scott and his comrades were destined to be present at Appomattox Court House on April 9 when Lee surrendered.

Chapter 13

THE FALL OF RICHMOND AND VICTORY AT LAST, SPRING/SUMMER OF 1865

G ordon was assigned to duty as military governor of the District of Eastern Virginia on February 11. He was not happy about it, but as was his habit, he accepted it. It was the equivalent of becoming the mayor of Norfolk, or perhaps more correctly, the absolute ruler. He had control of all phases of government, commerce and law and order. Still carrying out the inquiry, he soon found himself pushed to the limit. He was discovering new wrongdoing every day, including much illegal trade in cotton. One of his first actions was to clamp down on all trade with the Confederates. This action upset many people in the district, but he had Grant's full support.[96]

Meanwhile, Union forces were on the move on all fronts. Like the jaws of a giant vise, Grant's forces to the north and Sherman's to the south were closing in on Lee and his army. Sherman had moved through the Carolinas and left Charleston in ruins. And Sheridan, who had been operating in the Shenandoah with the Union cavalry, was closing in from the north.

Gordon's health improved steadily, and he applied himself energetically to his new job, demonstrating considerable administrative and organizational skill. It was the same characteristic that had served him so well designing and putting together a regiment at the outset of the war. Near the end of March, it was rumored that he would soon be given a field command leading a division. For months he had longed to get back to into action somehow and was now hopeful. Secretary of War Edwin Stanton, who was in the Norfolk area, reviewed the troops of the Army of the James with Grant. He visited

Gordon in his office. When Gordon inquired about his new assignment, Stanton's reply was a terrible disappointment:

> *No, you are not to be relieved. I fixed that matter with Generals Grant and Ord last night. You are doing too much good here, and we can not afford to lose you; you are doing better work here than if you were commanding a corps or division in the field, for you are stopping supplies from going to the enemy, and Hartsuff* [who was to take my place] *would have matters all mixed up in a short time.*[97]

The words of approval were gratifying, but it was not what he wanted to hear. He was given assurances that when local problems here were solved he would be relieved from this post. Although frustrated, he went back to work. One of the many things he had to deal with was a constant flow of deserters. They told stories of scarce rations, lack of ammunition and general low morale in the Confederate forces. Gordon, like Shepley before him, had charge of the civil fund, monies collected from taxes, licenses, polls, fees, permits, fines and rents paid by the government—the same monies that the civil authorities would receive in the normal course of events. Whereas Butler and Shepley had used these funds as their personal piggy bank, Gordon assiduously kept records of every dime collected and ensured that the funds were applied to the general welfare of the populace. A consensus was growing that the war's end was near.

President Lincoln came down to Norfolk from Washington at this time, and Secretary of State William Seward was in town, as well, with a delegation of foreign dignitaries. More or less by sheer coincidence, they all showed up at Gordon's headquarters on the same day, March 29 or 30.[98] Admiral Farragut accompanied the president. At the time, Gordon had a few Boston visitors of his own, including his wife, and they all had a cordial social visit in Gordon's office that afternoon. The president and his party stayed in the area, in expectation of the enemy's surrender.

Lee and his Army of Northern Virginia were really the only sizable Confederate force left. There was a remnant of the Army of Tennessee, commanded by General Joseph Johnston nearby, and they had been opposing Sherman as he advanced north. On April 1, in a desperation move, Lee attempted a breakout from Petersburg so that he could link up with Johnston. The attempt failed and simply resulted in more heavy losses.

On the morning of April 3, Gordon received a telegram advising that units of the Army of the James had entered the city of Richmond. He wrote of that day:

> *I cannot describe my feelings…I was at my office; and there the message was received—"authentic beyond doubt" it said. I put the telegram in my pocket and rushed on to the street. An officer spoke to me and I replied "We have Richmond!" In a moment I was with Admiral Farragut. He could hardly contain himself at the news. In his hand he held a copy of my dispatch. Could this news be true—the Admiral doubted. But his wife did not; she was jubilant…I returned to my office. A boat was ordered to be in readiness to convey the Admiral and myself to Richmond that night. Everything that could be turned out I commanded to parade the streets of Norfolk, with music, flags, and cheers…The city was wild with excitement.* [99]

Gordon was a man not given to impulses, but in the present circumstance he could not help himself. Probably with some urging from Admiral Farragut, he determined to go to Richmond to be an eyewitness to its fall. This man, whose whole life was characterized by strict discipline and adherence to protocol, threw caution to the winds and, with Farragut, hatched a plan:

> *At eleven o'clock at night, we were on the boat, steaming up the James. Of those who accompanied me there were, of officers, Admiral Farragut, my staff, Colonel Martindale, and Majors Stackpole and Binney; of ladies there were Mrs. Gordon and two ladies from Boston.* [100]

Gordon had arranged for saddled horses to be aboard. As they pulled out of the harbor at Norfolk, they saw the president's steamer, the *River Queen*, at anchor nearby. They hoped to beat him to Richmond! After getting as far up the James as was safely possible (the river was mined in many places), they debarked. Leaving the ladies behind, they mounted their horses and rode past abandoned fortifications into the city itself. Apparently the admiral had some difficulty, which caused Gordon to remark, "A sailor on horseback is not the man he is on his own quarter-deck." [101]

At ten o'clock in the morning, they entered the city limits. Gordon described the scene:

We made our way through dirty and tortuous streets, by the ashes of countless houses, and burning timbers, by household goods and furniture, and multitudes of men and women gazing hopelessly at the wreck and ruin, down the main avenue and into the square…Here we found General Weitzel. He had established his headquarters at the house and home of Jefferson Davis.[102] The lower part of the house was roomy and imposing. When Weitzel entered he was met by Davis's servants with the announcement that their master had told them that the Union commander would probably occupy the house, and that they must treat him well. The Rebel President's wines had been preserved, and in his parlor we drank to the health of the fugitive ruler of the Confederacy. As a memento I took away a group of bronze and wood, representing a bald eagle being strangled by a crocodile. It was thus, I suppose that the United States were to be throttled in an attempt to enslave the South. We were joined [later] in the parlor by the ladies. They were the first [ladies] to enter Richmond after its capture.[103]

Rather than return to the spot where they debarked, they commandeered a Rebel steamer in the city, boarded and headed downstream. An hour or

Richmond, capital of the Confederate States, shown in ruins following its capture, April 2, 1865. *Courtesy of the Library of Congress, LC-DIG-ppmsca-08230.*

A small gilded sculpture taken from the Confederate Executive Mansion in Richmond by General Gordon on April 4, 1865. It shows an alligator rising up to throttle an eagle, signifying the South defeating the North. *Courtesy of the Massachusetts Historical Society. Full citation in bibliography.*

so later, much to their satisfaction, they saw the president's steamer coming upstream. They had beaten him and his party into Richmond, but they had neglected to lower the Stars and Bars on their commandeered boat. As a result, they were almost attacked! After greetings with the president and his party, they went on their way back to Norfolk.

Five days later, on April 9, 1865, Lee surrendered at Appomattox. On April 11, Gordon received a telegram from Lincoln requesting information regarding the imprisonment of Butler's associates.[104] Gordon promptly sent a reply, explaining the facts and saying that General Grant had approved his actions. That seemed to end the matter, but Butler was not done.

Four days later, on April 14, the awful news of Lincoln's assassination reached Gordon. The nation was plunged into mourning.

Chapter 14

FINAL MILITARY DUTIES AND A RETURN
TO CIVILIAN LIFE, SUMMER/FALL OF 1865

G ordon summed up his feelings at this time in a letter to his mother:[105]

Headquarters, District of Virginia,
Norfolk, Va., April 11, 1865

My Dear Mother,

    Long before this letter reaches you, the glad news of peace will have been tonic to your ears. It is almost impossible to realize it, to know what to say, or do but so it is.

    ...I am so moved by conflicting emotions that I do not think I am myself. I have for four years given myself up so entirely to the war, have entered into it with all my body, soul, and strength that I feel as one who had lost the main spring of action.

    I feel so unnaturally and so grievously disappointed, too, that I was ordered to this point when the accomplishment of what I had labored so hard to achieve was won that it will take me some little time to recover.

    I know the world's opinion of our deeds is but of little moment, that applause and glory are short lived and are of no moment when mortal man is attacked with a severe cholic, but yet so silly are we that we are all disappointment if any toad jumps higher in the puddle than we do.

    I think now we shall return to the pursuits of peace at once. I imagine my occupation here is gone. Susie will return home, and I shall look street to street to see where next to pitch my tent. But yet it may be some time before that time comes, for there may be much military arrangement of the conquered country. I suppose now Framingham is moved into wildness by the news.

What induced Train to sell his house. Where is the foolish man going? If he wished to avail himself of the fortunes that are to be made in this country, he might have left his home F. to await his return. I think I may come home to see you too, if I don't come to remain. And in the meantime with much love to you and Robert, I am your loving son,

George
I am glad Harry is safe. G.H.

His "jumping toad" metaphor expresses his disappointment that disease and other bad breaks prevented him from achieving more honor on the field of battle. Still, the Rebels were vanquished, and his beloved country was whole again. He had reason to feel much pride in the part he had played.

In his present role, there was no letup in his responsibilities even if hostilities had ended. In the district of Virginia, as throughout the country, it required much work to transition back to a peacetime basis. In some areas, though not here, remnants of the Rebel armies fought on for a few weeks, but by early May all had laid down their arms. Jefferson Davis was captured on May 10 and brought back to Norfolk in irons to be held for a time under Gordon's authority at Fort Monroe. Provisions had to be made for the thousands of indigent former slaves who came daily into the city. The fabric of a civil administration had to be rebuilt. Thousands of former Confederate soldiers had to be screened before returning to civilian life. Sometime in May, while engaged in these activities, he received a communication from a West Point classmate who had joined the Rebels. He described their meeting:[106]

My classmate and roommate at West Point, a paroled Rebel officer just from Mobile, sent his card to me in Norfolk. When he appeared I recognized him in a moment, though he wore a shabby suit of a civilian,[107] but my impulse to greet him warmly was checked by his downward and repellant glance, as if he were averse to showing a cordial feeling for his foe. As if apologizing for his call he said:

Rebel: I have come, sir, because I am in trouble.

Gordon: Be seated…You could not have called upon one who could be more glad to relieve you.

Rebel: I want…to go to my wife and child. I am a beggar and want work—an opportunity to earn something to live on in the future. But for the present I want money.

Gordon: I see in you…my old classmate and friend. I find you suffering and in want, and you shall have money and all the privileges I can give. But tell me, how could you, though Southern born, find it in your heart to raise your hand against the old flag?

Rebel: Don't talk of it…

Poor fellow, I thought.

Scenes such as this were repeated many times over throughout the South in the months that followed. Lincoln had hoped for a reconciliation and a more liberal approach to bringing Southern states back into the Union, but it was going to be difficult. Some of the more radical members of the Congress were bent on punishing the South and forcing reform on its people, and most Southern congressmen were still resistant to change.

In late May, the Union armies converged on Washington for a grand review. Gordon's old regiment, his beloved 2nd Regiment, Massachusetts Volunteer Infantry, passed in review as part of Sherman's Army of Georgia. Of the roughly one thousand men who had assembled at Brook Farm in May 1861, fewer than one hundred remained. Of the original officers, there were only four.[108] They had been in numerous major battles since their separation from Gordon: Chattanooga, Atlanta and with Sherman in his march through Georgia and the Carolinas. They had hoped there could be a parade through Boston, but the War Department forbade it. They were mustered out at Readville and went their separate ways.

Eventually, Gordon turned his concern to the matter of his own future. He began making plans to return to Massachusetts and civilian life. He and Lizzie had had little time together since they had married. Still bothered by less-than-robust health, he took a leave of absence in June and came home, bringing with him the retinue of servants, staff and baggage that he had carried with him throughout the war, as well as his fine horse, Ashby. At home, there was no fanfare for those returning—no parades, no celebrations. The country was war-weary and wanted to put it all behind.

Returning to Virginia, he had much to do to wind up his responsibilities in the district. In early August, he received a promotion to (brevet) major general, retroactive to April 9. On August 24, he was mustered out and headed home for the last time. He was soon back in his law office at Court Street in Boston, gathering up the pieces of his former practice. Back in Framingham, one of his first actions was to make some changes to the big barn to provide a suitable home for Ashby. This gallant horse that he had found on the battlefield in the Shenandoah Valley had been his constant companion in the war years. Wherever Gordon went, Ashby went, be it

The Gordon homestead, circa 1900. It was to this place, which Gordon loved so much, that he returned at the end of the war. In the background is seen the barn, in which Ashby, the general's trusted horse, lived out his days after the war. With Lizzie, his mother and brother, Gordon would remain here the rest of his life. *Courtesy of the Framingham History Center.*

the valley, the islands off Charleston, the Mississippi, Mobile Bay or eastern Virginia. They were inseparable.

> *I brought him to a quiet country home within twenty miles of Boston. In a comfortable stable with a box stall, with every provision made for his comfort, "old Ashby" passed a tranquil life. In his peaceful home, and with kind treatment, his disposition became gentler.*[109]

As he slowly worked back into legal circles in Boston, there was a sadness in the air. So many of the bright young men he had worked with were gone. Slowly, his new life began to unfold. He and Lizzie were happy together in

The national colors, originally presented to Gordon and his regiment in June 1861, were returned to the Massachusetts Statehouse on December 22, 1865. They had been carried in every battle throughout the war by the regiment. *Courtesy of the Commonwealth of Massachusetts Art Commission, cw-02a-1987.360.*

the family home in Framingham. Mother Gordon was in her seventies but was still very active and a force in their lives. Henry Scott, now a colonel in the 4th Massachusetts Cavalry, stayed in Virginia as part of the occupation forces in Richmond and was finally mustered out in November.

Soon after returning home, probably in the fall, Gordon met with Governor Andrew and presented him with the little sculpture of the crocodile and eagle, which he had taken from Jefferson Davis's executive mansion in Richmond. The governor graciously thanked him both for the gift and for his service. The feud that had complicated their relationship throughout the war was put to rest. In December, representatives from all of the state's volunteer militia units met at the statehouse on Beacon Hill and deposited their regimental flags there. The flag of the 2nd Massachusetts was "pierced and torn, riddled with shot and shell."[110] Gordon attended the ceremony.

In Framingham, life began to return to normal. However, for some, it would never be the same. The war's cost in blood and treasure was being counted. In the annual report for the year ending March 1, 1866, the town clerk made an accounting. The amounts expended were as follows: in bounties and recruiting, $33,828.86; for aid to families of soldiers, $20,456.87; and the amount of individual subscriptions for recruiting and bounty funds, $29,142.50—a grand total of $83,428.23. The clerk reported on the work of the Framingham Ladies Auxiliary of the Sanitary Commission, listing hundreds of articles of clothing, bandages, bedding and underwear, which they made and sent to the troops, being careful to mention that there were groups from all three villages in town who contributed. Finally, he listed the names of 402 persons credited to the town under the various calls, including 19 who were killed or died from war-related causes. Subsequent research by Civil War historian Tom A. Ellis has shown that a total of 530 persons of this town, native or by residence, served and that 52 were killed or died of war-related causes. In the 1860 federal census, Framingham's population was 4,250, give or take a few. When we consider demographics, the numbers suggest that virtually every able-bodied man in town, between the ages of eighteen and thirty, served.

By 1867, the town fathers began to make plans for a memorial to honor those who had served and fallen. Many towns in the commonwealth were in the process of erecting monuments, statues or monoliths with names inscribed. The people of Framingham wanted a "living memorial," something

Memorial Hall and Library, completed in 1873. The people of Framingham erected this building to honor the men of their town who had fought and died in the war. Following Gordon's death, Lizzie donated money for the construction of an addition to the rear of the building in the general's honor. *Courtesy of* Framingham Illustrated, *1880.*

that would be used and would serve as a constant reminder of the sacrifices made. They settled on the idea of a great hall combined with a library. In 1872, construction was begun, and in 1873, the completed structure was opened and dedicated. Given the name Memorial Hall originally, it would be known later as the Edgell Memorial Library.

Chapter 15
EARLY POSTWAR YEARS, 1866–1872

During the winter season, Lizzie and George sometimes stayed in Boston and left Mother Gordon and brother Robert at the house in Framingham with a handyman caretaker and servants. As a war hero of sorts, Gordon was sought after to lecture on his experiences. Often he was asked to officiate at ceremonies relating to the war, such as dedications of monuments. He and Lizzie were welcome guests at social events in the city. Most of his clients were in Boston as well. All of these activities tended to keep them in town, but when the warm breezes of spring began to blow along the banks of the Sudbury River, back they came to the place they called home.

In May 1866, on the fifth anniversary of the formation of the 2nd Regiment, a group of comrades from its ranks gathered at Brook Farm, or Camp Andrew. Alonzo Quint described the scene:

> *They paused at the entrance where the guard had once challenged the visitor. The home was unchanged since the sentinel had ceased to walk his post before headquarters. The marks of the little trenches about the first tents, the rains had not yet washed away. Here and there were found a few scraps of decayed canvas. And slight remnants of tent pins. The flag-staff still stood, from which no flag had flown since the summer day when the banner of the Second had left it. Recollections of Dwight and Sargent, of Savage, Abbott, and Cary, Goodwin, Mudge, Williams, Segwick, Hill, Shaw Robeson, Choate and Perkins,—all dead for their country, and of the hundreds of the*

brave and faithful in the ranks gone with them, were fresh in memory. The comrades plucked some bright spring flowers, and left the plot in silence.[111]

A move was soon afoot to form an organization of veterans of the regiment, and Gordon would play a significant role by serving as its president for several years.

The law practice was slow to build up, and Gordon began to consider taking a job with the federal government to supplement his income. Discussing the matter with Henry Wilson and other associates, he learned of an opening for U.S. marshal for the district of Massachusetts. Ulysses S. Grant wrote to President Andrew Johnson strongly recommending Gordon for a civil appointment. In August, word came that President Johnson had appointed him to the position, but there was what seemed like a minor complication. Since it was summer and the Congress was not in session, Gordon's would have to be a recess appointment, to be approved by the Senate in its next session in March 1867.

The reader will recall that a year earlier, in 1865, General Butler's military career had ended ignominiously when Grant relieved him of duty following the failed Fort Fisher expedition and his implication in a scheme to trade contraband of war with Lee's army while in charge of the District of Eastern Virginia. Butler was a well-connected politician, if not a very good military strategist, and was not going to take this without a fight. He went to Lincoln, pleading that he and the others had been falsely accused and badly treated by both Gordon and Grant. Lincoln promptly sent Gordon a telegram demanding a full explanation of the facts surrounding the incarceration of Butler's associates. It was dated April 11, 1865, and read as follows:[112]

Brig. Gen. Geo. H. Gordon

Norfolk, Va

Send to me at once a full statement as to the cause or causes for which, and by authority of what Tribunal, Geo. W. Lane, Chas. Whitlock, Ezra Baker, J.M. Renshaw, and others, are restrained of their liberty. Do this promptly and fully.

Lincoln

Gordon's immediate reply spelled out the details of the case and referenced General Grant as the authority for his actions. Tragically, just three days later, Lincoln was assassinated. Washington was thrown into turmoil, and Lincoln's inquiry died along with him. However, over the next few months, Butler worked the halls of Congress trying to discredit the commission's report. The House of Representatives conducted its own investigation but stopped short of making a final report.

In the fall of 1866, Butler ran successfully for a seat in the House of Representatives and waited for an opportunity to take his revenge. This was the backdrop against which Gordon was appointed U.S. marshal. When Congress convened in March 1867, Butler called on all of his connections in an effort to defeat the appointment, and in the end it was rejected. His influence was probably not the only factor. It should be noted that Congress was very hostile toward President Johnson and probably would have rejected any of his appointments. Gordon now felt that his reputation had been tarnished. He would respond.

The year 1868 was one for presidential elections, and Gordon learned that Butler was running for reelection to the House of Representatives on the Republican ticket. This was too much for him. He felt so strongly that the man was unfit to hold public office that he vowed to work for Butler's defeat, even though he seldom became involved in politics. He became active in Boston's Republican party and gave a rousing speech endorsing Ulysses S. Grant at Faneuil Hall in June of that same year.[113] However, he campaigned against fellow Republican Butler in his own district by laying out for audiences, much in the manner of a prosecutor, the details of Butler's crimes (as he saw them), and defending his own record.[114] In a speech in Salem, Massachusetts, for example, he spelled out the charges:[115]

New York Times, 24 Oct., 1868

GEN. B.F. BUTLER

His Military Career—Supplies for the
Rebels—Speech by Gen. Gordon in Salem

Gen. Geo. H. Gordon addressed the citizens of Salem Friday night in
Mechanics Hall. We report the extracts of his address, given below, from

the Boston Advertiser, in which the speech is published in full. After a little preliminary the General said:

And since Gen. BUTLER has, in a public manner, offered to resign as a candidate for the high office to which he aspires to, if Gen. GRANT will invite him to do so, I now present for his consideration the following letter from the General, written more than one year after Butler's military career had terminated to show whether Gen. GRANT is or is not deeply interested in Gen. BUTLER's success in the Fifth Congressional District. In a letter on file in the public archives in Washington, dated July 4, 1865, Gen. GRANT uses the following language: "While the Union Army was holding LEE in Richmond and Petersburg, I found the latter was receiving supplies either through the inefficiency or with the permission of the officer selected by Gen. BUTLER for the command of Norfolk through Albemarle and Chesapeake Canal. Knowing _____ _____ [116] to be honest and capable I attached him to the Army of the James to take that command, knowing that no persuasion could make him swerve from his duty." I shall now show you that the supplies GRANT learns LEE was receiving through the inefficiency or permission of an officer selected by General BUTLER, were supplied to the rebel army within and from the Department commanded by B.F. BUTLER for the sole profit and advantage of a ring, of which BENJAMIN F. BUTLER was the head, Fisher A. Hildreth of Lowell, BUTLER's brother-in-law, chief manager, and one George W. Lane and J.B. Sanborn, subordinates. The testimony taken under oath, which establishes the facts claimed…are to be found in a published report of a Committee of the House of Representatives of the Thirty Eighth Congress…and also in a report of a military commission ordered to investigate the same trade from the Department of Virginia and North Carolina, while commanded by B.F. BUTLER.

In a speech in Newburyport, Massachusetts, about the same time, he ended with:

You are to judge, Gentlemen, whether such a man should represent your district beyond the time which expires the 4th of March next. My duty is done. The honor, the welfare, the life of the State is in the hands of the people. Let each citizen so live and act and vote as if upon him alone rested the responsibility for the nation's life.

Despite Gordon's efforts, Butler was reelected in 1868 and several times thereafter. For these two men, the die had been cast. They would remain enemies for the rest of their lives. In a sense, Gordon had the last word in the present circumstance. Grant was elected and took office in 1869, and a year later Gordon was offered a choice of appointments in his administration, either as consul to Egypt or as commissioner of Internal Revenue in the 7th District, Massachusetts. Gordon opted for the latter and was quickly confirmed. Grant signed the commission on February 16, 1870. Butler did not choose to oppose the wishes of a president of his own party. Gordon held that position for several years at a salary of $3,000 per year—about the same rate of pay as a senator. In 1872, Grant ran for reelection with a new running mate, Gordon's old friend Henry Wilson, and they won easily.

Chapter 16
PEACEFUL DAYS IN FRAMINGHAM AND SETTING THE RECORD STRAIGHT, 1872–1886

Life settled into a quiet routine for the Gordons. Sometimes, on a summer's morn, he would saddle up Ashby to go at a leisurely pace up Grove Street and into the fields and forests there. The horse's gait had slowed, but he still stood erect and alert. Often they came upon Frank Bowditch out riding one of his fine thoroughbreds. This was the same Bowditch who had presented the colors to the newly formed 2nd Regiment at Brook Farm back in June 1861. The son of a wealthy Bostonian, he had recently purchased the old Buckminster Farm, a tract of about one thousand acres, and built himself a mansion there. He was turning the property into the American equivalent of an English country estate, complete with tenant farmers, livestock, crops and, for entertainment, fox hunting. He and Gordon shared a love of fine horses and soon became close friends, often riding together over the many trails throughout Millwood, as Bowditch had chosen to name the place.

Eventually, Ashby's time had come. Gordon told the story himself:

> On Monday, the eighteenth of May, 1874, I was aroused early in the morning with the news that my poor old horse was in great pain, and would not eat. I lost not a moment in applying remedies, sending in the meantime for one more skilled.
>
> Everything was tried but nothing seemed to lessen the pain in the stomach…there was the seat of the pain. Beseechingly would this intelligent animal look, first at one side, then at the other, then at us appealing for

help…Early in the afternoon, it became evident that the noble animal must die. He was lying down in the soft grass some distance from the house, only occasionally lifting his head in an uneasy manner…As I saw this splendid frame stretched helplessly upon the earth, so exhausted by the agony he had suffered that he could but feebly lift his head, as I saw that bright eye half closed, and heard that quick breath as it came through that great nostril, as I saw my friend, my companion of so many years, so helpless before me, strength gone, muscles feeble,—as the memory of all this dear companion had been came over me, I shed such tears as I thought never to shed again. Kneeling by him I stroked his face, and then gently raising his head, coaxed him to attempt to rise. The rain was beginning to fall and I wished to shelter him, and also that he might breathe his last in the old stable where he had stood so long. Putting forth all his dying force, and obedient to a call that he knew had never been made but in love, he staggered to his feet. Gently I led him, tottering and reeling, to his stable, where a soft bed had been prepared. I covered him with blankets to retain as long as possible the ebbing life. It was now two o'clock.

For seven hours "Ashby" hardly moved from the spot where I had placed him in his stall; there was but little restlessness, though his breathing became more rapid, and labored as the night came on… [A]*t quarter before nine at night he fell dead upon the floor. I heard the rattle of death in his throat as tenderly I closed his eyes. Then turning from him, gently, lovingly, I said: "My poor old friend, my dear old companion, I have tried to be as faithful to you as you have been true and constant to me."*

[Ashby was laid to rest] *under the green sod in the orchard where he has so many times played without restraint, in sight of the home that has so gently cared for him and under the apple trees…whose blossoms now whiten his grave.*[117]

As the decade of the 1870s progressed, the general turned his attention to his own place in history and to some unresolved issues associated with the war. He spent hours at home in his office, researching and writing about his experiences, both good and bad. Although he had no children of his own, he wanted future generations to know of his service. One priority was to correct the falsehoods and slanders that Butler had spread about him. But that was not his only purpose. He wanted to present his own view of events—about certain battles and about certain individuals. One of these was the case of

General Fitz John Porter. Gordon was deeply disturbed by the treatment that Porter had received and was determined to do something about it.

The case was related to events that had occurred during the Second Battle of Bull Run (Manassas), when both Gordon and Porter were part of Pope's Army of Virginia. The battle was a defeat for the Union forces, and Pope subsequently accused Porter of misconduct and disobeying orders. He was tried by court-martial, found guilty, stripped of his rank and dismissed from the service. His life was ruined. Gordon served alongside Porter at Bull Run, as well as in other campaigns, and considered him a good, capable man. To Gordon, it was another example of a high-ranking officer trying to shift blame for his own failures to a subordinate, and since the close of the war, he had been on a crusade to exonerate Porter. He was not alone in this; many people, in and out of government, shared his convictions.

In typical lawyerlike fashion, Gordon proceeded to sift through thousands of government documents, official records of the war and testimony given at Porter's trial.[118] He built a rebuttal of the charges, wrote to members of the Senate and House with whom he had some influence, circulated petitions and was instrumental in the formation of a board of review in the mid-1870s, ten years after the fact. In 1878, the board ruled that Porter's actions during the Second Battle of Bull Run had actually saved Pope from an even greater defeat. He was exonerated, his dismissal from the army was revoked and he was restored to the rank of colonel.

Gordon's interest in the history of the war, and his own writings on the subject, brought him into contact with John Codman Ropes,[119] a wealthy Bostonian and student of military history. Ropes had a special interest in the Civil War, and in February 1876, he invited a group of twelve former Union officers to a meeting at which he proposed the formation of a group dedicated to preserving the history of the war. Gordon was among those invited to attend. Out of that meeting was founded the Military Historical Society of Massachusetts. Gordon served as its first president and was a frequent speaker at its meetings.

He was also a member of the Massachusetts Commandery of the Military Order of the Loyal Legion of the United States (MOLLUS), an organization of former Union officers dedicated to the protection and preservation of the Union.

Gordon, now in his mid-fifties, was having some new health problems. In retrospect, the symptoms were suggestive of heart trouble. He was spending

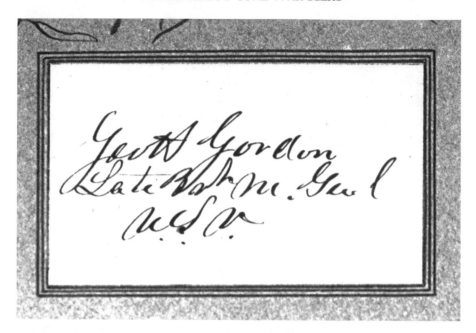

Above: Autograph, circa 1880. It reads "Geo. H. Gordon, Late Bvt. M. Gen'l, U.S.V." *Courtesy of MOLLUS-MA.*

Left: General Gordon, now looking elderly, at home in Framingham, circa 1880. *Courtesy of MOLLUS-MA.*

more time at home now, working several hours each day on his memoirs, busy with correspondence and speaking engagements. More and more he was in Framingham, but he still took the train into Boston as work required.

Throughout the 1870s, Gordon was a regular attendee at Framingham's town meetings, and when he spoke his opinions carried considerable weight. For some time, he had spoken about the poor condition of the bridge across the Sudbury River by his home and had advocated replacing it. A bridge committee was formed, with Gordon a member. They brought forward a proposal to replace the old wooden bridges here and on Main Street near the old burying ground with new, modern structures made of iron. Some townspeople felt that this was extravagant, but he argued persuasively that in the long run the durability of this material justified the expense. He was appointed to oversee the project, and it was completed in one year—on time and under budget, with every penny expended carefully accounted for in typical Gordon fashion.[120] Time proved him right—the Main Street bridge would last for one hundred years! The other was swept away in the 1950s by hurricane rains after eighty years of service.

In 1880, his first book, *History of the Campaign of the Army of Virginia, under John Pope, Brigadier General, from Cedar Mountain to Alexandria, 1862*, was published. Perhaps it is not a coincidence that he wrote first about this period. It contains an eloquent defense of General Fitz John Porter's actions during Second Manassas.

The general and his wife had no children of their own, but they enjoyed visits by cousin and brother Henry B. Scott, who by now was married and had a family. Toward the end of the war, Scott had struck off on his own, taking command of a Massachusetts cavalry unit in January 1865. He saw action near Appomattox and achieved the rank of colonel before the end of the war. Since then, he had tried his hand at raising cotton in Florida for a time before moving to Iowa, where he had a long and prosperous career with the Burlington Railroad. His two oldest sons, Henry R. and George C., had fond memories of the old general. From time to time, the Scott family would return to Framingham for visits. At a meeting of Framingham's Historical Society in 1939, Henry recalled one of these when he and his brother were eight or nine years old:[121]

Despite his rather severe military carriage we boys liked our Uncle George.[122]
He would come out on an earlier train, sometimes when we were here on a

visit, and with our aunt we could drive to the Centre Station to meet him. Then we would go for a drive. In those days at the brook crossings, there was a little ford at one side down and across the brook. Uncle George drove the horse down to the brook and let him stop. And then he called "Now, Georgie," and my brother walked out on the shaft, and let down the horse's check rein so that he could drink.

In the evening our Uncle would read to us from Pickwick Papers, which was great fun. Sometimes we got into trouble. My brother remembers the occasion when he and I cut sticks, inserted them in green apples and hurled the apples—alas! crash through a window in the barn. This was too much and the General went after Georgie with the horse whip. As my brother ran the General overtook him with his longer legs and laid the whip on the youngster's legs. But no matter what our deviltries, when Uncle George got seated comfortably in his easy chair, after supper, he was always ready to read to us from Frank on the Lower Mississippi, or tell us some tale of the war.

In 1880, the general, now fifty-seven, and Mrs. Gordon were enjoying a life that included extended vacation trips to the Pacific coast, to the White Mountains of New Hampshire and so on. He did a little farming as well. Again, quoting his young cousin, Henry:

When the cattle show came around in September,[123] [the General and Frank Bowditch] *usually had a bet up as to which could raise the largest pumpkin, or as to who could best the other in the prizes for grapes.*

And further:

Young people, even though they see a man in the familiar ways of home life, often fail to get at the deep underlying principles and character of the man. He was more likely to throw some jest at his wife or at us than to parade sentiment or disclose the bulwarks of his character. But his wife knew too well that his joke often cloaked some incipient attack of the disease which was fast laying hold upon him. And as for us boys, we never appreciated the strength and nobility of his character.

In 1882, his second book, *A War Diary of Events in the War of the Great Rebellion, 1863–1865,* was ready for publication. Again, it would seem there was a purpose in taking events out of order. In this volume, he refuted many of the falsehoods Butler had spread about him and furthermore documented in great detail, and with references to official reports, the charges he had made against Butler. Ironically, Butler was elected governor of Massachusetts that same year.

These were sad years for the family, as Mother Gordon passed away in 1881 at the fine old age of ninety-one, and brother Robert died suddenly in 1882. This left the general and Mrs. Gordon alone, with a few members of staff in the big old house at Gordon's Corner. Gordon's own health steadily declined as well. He seldom traveled to Boston now and contented himself with local affairs and speaking engagements. His third and final book, *Brook Farm to Cedar Mountain in the War of the Great Rebellion, 1861–1862*, published in 1883, completed the record of his years of service in the war.

In February 1886, he was still able enough to present a seminar at Lowell Institute on the Battle of Antietam, but by springtime, he was having more difficulty. Together with Lizzie, he traveled to Carlsbad in Europe, where he "took the baths," hoping for relief from the heart trouble, but he experienced little benefit. They returned in early August, and he was confined to home. During the last week in August, things reached a crisis. Specialists from Boston were called in, but there was little to be done. Although only sixty-three years of age, the rigors of war and disease contracted in the camps had overtaken him. On Monday, August 30, he passed away.

Mrs. Gordon entrusted Frank Bowditch with funeral arrangements. A brief service was held at the family home. Officiating were Reverend Brooke Hereford of the Arlington Street Church in Boston, where Gordon often attended during the winter months, and Reverend Charles A. Humphreys of First Parish of Framingham. Pallbearers, all original members of his 2nd Massachusetts Infantry, were General A.B. Underwood, Colonel James Francis, Major John A. Fox, General S.M. Quincy, Colonel C.P. Horton, Chaplain Alonzo H. Quint and Captain G.P. Bangs. Also serving was Dr. Z.B. Adams. Other dignitaries included representatives from the Loyal Legion; a number of leading citizens from Framingham; Judges Charles Devens and Charles Allen of the Massachusetts Supreme Court; the Honorable John C. Ropes of the Military Historical Society of Massachusetts; and finally Woodward Emery, who had shared an office with Gordon in Boston in recent days. He was laid to rest in his general's uniform at the family burial plot in Edgell Grove Cemetery.

Above: The Gordon family monument at Edgell Grove Cemetery, Framingham. Buried here are Gordon, his wife Maria (Lizzie), his mother Elizabeth, his brother and several other family members. His individual marker is indicated by the small flag. *Courtesy of Edgell Grove Cemetery. Photo by the author.*

Left: Marble bust of Gordon, by noted sculptor Daniel C. French, executed in 1887. On display at the Framingham History Center. Funds for its creation were donated by veterans of the 2nd Regiment, Massachusetts Volunteer Infantry, as well as citizens of Framingham. *Courtesy of the Framingham History Center. Photo by Austin Daniells.*

Soon after his death, a group of citizens in Framingham, headed by Reverend Humphreys of First Parish, embarked on a drive to raise funds to procure a bust of the general for the Memorial Hall Library at Framingham Centre. Joined by members of the 2nd Massachusetts Regiment Association and other colleagues of the general, sufficient funds were soon raised. Noted sculptor Daniel C. French of Concord produced a handsome image of the general from Italian marble, which was on display in Boston for several weeks. In November 1888, a grateful community installed the bust in its final resting place at the library, where it still stands. Mrs. Gordon further memorialized her husband by donating funds for a new wing on that building.

CLOSING THOUGHTS

To capture the full measure of a man in a few paragraphs is an impossible task, but we will attempt here a brief summary. Of Gordon, it can be said that he was a man of the highest moral integrity—a good man. He was a patriot with an unflinching devotion to duty and country. A stern man, almost cold at times, he set the same high standard for his troops. From his early war experiences, he understood that, in war, there is no substitute for sound training and discipline, so he demanded these qualities in his officers and men.

He had to deal with much adversity throughout his life. He grew up poor and without a father. He suffered serious wounds in the Mexican-American War. He had just begun to establish himself in a good law practice in Boston when the Civil War broke out, and his sense of duty compelled him to leave it behind. He suffered from poor leadership in the ranks of his superiors. Many historians have labeled Generals Banks and Pope as among the poorest of Union generals, and Butler's performance was controversial on and off the battlefield. Then there was disease. Gordon's struggles with typhoid and malaria made it impossible for him to fulfill his aspirations for battlefield honors in the latter part of the war.

Still, he had his triumphs. In the early years of the war, he distinguished himself in several major battles, Antietam being the most notable. And he demonstrated great skill as a military administrator in the District of Eastern Virginia and in the investigations he conducted there.

He had his failings. He tried to hold others, especially his superiors, to his own strict standards, and when they fell short, he sometimes felt compelled to criticize publicly. In doing so, he always felt secure in the belief that he was in the right, but it often proved detrimental to his career.

Upon his death, he received many tributes. The 2nd Massachusetts Regiment Association, at its annual reunion of 1886, honored him. Later, the Massachusetts Commandery of the Military Order of the Loyal Legion (MOLLUS) issued its own tribute to him. Perhaps an excerpt from it gives us the best insight into the kind of person Gordon really was:

> *He who did more than any one man to organize, educate, discipline, and build up a command which was as we know regarded by many most competent to judge as a model volunteer regiment, has a lasting claim upon the gratitude of the country to whose volunteer soldiers that example was set at a moment when the national life trembled in the balance.*
>
> *To those who knew General Gordon simply as a military man, even to many who were brought into official relations with him, he often appeared cold and stern. Understandably his high sharp sense of military training and his unhesitating idea of duty, whether in himself or others, contributed to this appearance. But he was inflexibly just in his relation to all his subordinates of every rank, and those who even in the field, had some degree of personal intimacy with him, knew and recognized one of the kindest, and most generous natures. His ideal, however, was <u>duty</u>, and no sentiments were ever allowed to interfere with that ideal.*[124]

NOTES

REFERENCE	ABBREVIATION
Massachusetts Historical Society, Civil War Correspondence, Diaries and Journals, Microfilm Call Number P376, Reels 21–29	MHSC
Brook Farm to Cedar Mountain, in the War of the Great Rebellion, 1861–1862, by George H. Gordon	BFCM
History of the Campaign of the Army of Virginia, Under John Pope, Brigadier General, U.S.A., late Major General, U.S. Volunteers, from Cedar Mountain to Alexandria, 1862, by George H. Gordon	HCAV
A War Diary of Events in the War of the Great Rebellion, 1863–1865, by George H. Gordon	WDGR
The Record of the Second Massachusetts Infantry, 1861–1865, by Alonzo Quint	RSMI
The War of the Rebellion: A Compilation of the Records of the Union and Confederate Armies, Series I, edited by Robert N. Scott	OR
National Archives and Records Administration	NARA

Complete citations for these works are given in the bibliography.

CHAPTER 1

1. Private notes of Maria Scott Gordon, Framingham History Center.
2. NARA Publication Microcopy 688, Record Group 94, Charles W. Goodnow, February 12, 1839.
3. 1840 Federal Census.
4. See John Merriam's treatise on the academy, published in the *Framingham News*, October 28, 1937.
5. See note 1.

CHAPTER 2

6. MHSC, Letter, October 2, 1846.
7. Ibid., Letter, December 29, 1846.
8. Ibid., Diary, April 1847.
9. A major city on the national road between Vera Cruz and Mexico City.
10. A major city on this road.
11. General David Twiggs, commanded a division in Scott's army.
12. MHSC, Letter, April 19, 1847.
13. G.H. Gordon to Edgar Wheeler, Letter, November 1, 1847, from the private collection of Henry R. Scott (cousin).
14. MHSC, for Gordon's description of these escort missions, see letter, October 26, 1847.
15. The United States and Great Britain had by now settled their dispute over the area and established the forty-ninth parallel as the boundary between their lands, putting Fort Vancouver within the U.S. territory.
16. MHSC, Diary, 1850.
17. For more on this topic, see histories of Oregon.
18. MHSC, Oregon Diary, 1850.
19. MHSC, Special Order No. 60, Headquarters of the Army, August 19, 1853.

CHAPTER 3

20. See Boston City Directories for this period.
21. RSMI, 1.

CHAPTER 4

22. RSMI, 1.
23. Framingham Town Annual Report for the year ending March 1, 1862.
24. Duncan, *Blue Eyed Child of Fortune*, 167 and sources therein.
25. MHSC, Letter, July 8, 1861.
26. BFCM, 23–24.

CHAPTER 5

27. MHSC, Letter, July 16, 1861, Gordon speaks of "13,000 rebels under Col. [Joseph E.] Johnston, a former friend of mine."
28. BFCM, 259.
29. A brigade was usually three to five regiments, commanded by a brigadier general.
30. BFCM, Letter, October 7, 1861.
31. MHSC, Letter, October 24, 1861.
32. Ibid., Letter, December 11, 1861.
33. Robert Gould Shaw—he and Scott were classmates at Harvard, class of 1860.
34. MHSC, Letter, January 9, 1862.

CHAPTER 6

35. This was the 3rd Brigade, 1st Division, Banks's 5th Corps.
36. BFCM, 104.
37. Ibid., 168.
38. Ibid., 169.
39. Ibid., 195.
40. Ibid., 207.
41. OR, Series I.
42. BFCM, 141 ff.
43. Ralph Waldo Emerson Association deposit, Houghton Library, Harvard University, call number MS Am 1280 (1233), not to be reproduced in whole or in part without permission.

44. *Atlantic* magazine, "American Civilization," April 1862.

45. In the South, a slave was considered a piece of property, entirely analogous to any other material possession.

46. Winchester, Virginia, where the Union forces were victorious against the forces of Stonewall Jackson early in the Valley Campaign (Battle of Winchester).

CHAPTER 7

47. MHSC, Letter, July 16, 1862.

48. BFCM, 277.

49. For years after the war, there would be a dispute about who gave the order to stand and fight. Banks blamed Pope, and Pope blamed Banks. Gordon, writing about the battle years later, blamed Banks. He always felt that Banks had ordered the attack in hopes of avenging his earlier defeat at Jackson's hands in the Battle of Winchester, in complete disregard for the lives of his men.

50. BFCM, 315.

51. In late 1864, the Committee on the Conduct of the War, a watchdog group set up by Congress, did an investigation into the conduct of this battle, at which Banks and Pope alternately blamed each other and their subordinates for the failed attack.

52. HCAV, 39.

53. Ibid., 167.

54. Train, *Puritan's Progress*, 264.

CHAPTER 8

55. A particularly devastating type of shell called grape and canister, which showered the battlefield with shrapnel.

56. Train, *Puritan's Progress*, 268.

57. OR, Series I.

58. Train, *Puritan's Progress*, 268.

59. WDGR, 3.

60. MHSC, Letter, September 17, 1862.

CHAPTER 9

61. WDGR, 7.
62. RSMI, 55.
63. WDGR, 27.
64. Ibid., 38.
65. Ibid., 41.
66. A small town at the headwaters of the York River.
67. WDGR, 141.

CHAPTER 10

68. MHSC, Letter, September 12, 1861.
69. After the fall of the island, the army made an offer to Shaw's parents to retrieve his body and give him a proper burial. They declined, saying that he would want to be at rest with the men of his regiment.
70. OR, Series I.
71. Ibid., Series I, Volume 28, Part 2, 59.
72. WDGR, 224.
73. Ibid., 258.
74. Ibid., 259.
75. Ibid., 277.
76. Gordon gave a full account of this episode in a letter to the editor of the *Boston Daily Advertiser*, April 26, 1871. It was in response to charges made against him by arch rival Benjamin Butler.

CHAPTER 11

77. OR, Series I.
78. Mr. John Hay, Lincoln's private secretary.
79. A reference to Lincoln's Proclamation of Amnesty and Reconstruction.
80. WDGR, 289.
81. The Union Party Nominating Conference.
82. WDGR, 299.
83. Massachusetts Vital Records, 1864, Volume 172, 86.

84. WDGR, 306.
85. Ibid., 322.
86. The term "torpedoes" in this war referred to floating explosive charges in waterways.
87. WDGR, 350.

CHAPTER 12

88. WDGR, 350–52.
89. Ibid., 359.
90. Ibid., 355.
91. MHSC, Diary, 1864.
92. A reference to the home of his mother's sister, Maria (Ames) Chase, of Bullfinch Place, Boston.
93. WDGR, 368.
94. Ibid., 375.
95. From a speech given by George H. Gordon at Newburyport, Massachusetts, October 28, 1868.

CHAPTER 13

96. WDGR, 380.
97. Ibid., 383.
98. Ibid., 391.
99. Ibid., 392.
100. Ibid., 393.
101. Ibid., 394.
102. The Executive Mansion of the Confederacy.
103. WDGR, 395.
104. MHSC, Telegram, April 11, 1865.

CHAPTER 14

105. MHSC, Letter, April 11, 1865.

106. WDGR, 426.

107. The wearing of the Confederate officer's uniform was illegal at this time.

108. RSMI, 280.

109. BFCM, 141 ff.

110. RSMI, 292.

CHAPTER 15

111. Ibid., 293.

112. MHSC, see note 104.

113. *Boston Daily Advertiser*, June 12, 1868.

114. See, for example, "Speech of Gen. Geo. H. Gordon, at Newburyport, Mass., October 28, 1868," from the archives of the Framingham History Center.

115. Quote from the *New York Times*, October 24, 1867.

116. The omitted name is, in fact, George H. Gordon.

CHAPTER 16

117. BFCM, 147.

118. A complete account of Gordon's findings is given in his book *History of the Campaign of the Army of Virginia.*

119. Founder of the internationally known law firm of Ropes and Gray.

120. Framingham Town Annual Report, 1878, Report of the Bridge Committee.

121. *Framingham News*, "Through Civil War with Major General George H. Gordon," October 31, 1939.

122. Actually, first cousins, once removed.

123. Annual Fair of the Middlesex South Agricultural Society, held at Framingham.

CLOSING THOUGHTS

124. "Tribute to Major General George H. Gordon," read at the meeting of the Massachusetts Commandery, Military Order of the Loyal Legion of the United States, November 1, 1886, Gordon archive, Framingham History Center.

BIBLIOGRAPHY

Burton, E. Milby. *The Siege of Charleston, 1861–1865*. Columbia: University of South Carolina Press, 1970.

Cullum, George W., Brevet Major General. *Biographical Register of the U.S. Military Academy at West Point, N.Y. from its Establishment in 1802 to 1900*. Vol. 2. Third edition, revised and extended. Cambridge, MA: Houghton, Mifflin & Company, the Riverside Press, 1891.

Duncan, Russell, ed. *Blue Eyed Child of Fortune: Civil War Letters of Robert Gould Shaw*. Athens: University of Georgia Press, 1992.

Ellis, Thomas A.C. *Civil War Service of the Men and Women of Framingham, Massachusetts, 1861–1865*. Framingham, MA: Framingham Historical Society, 2000.

Gordon, George H. *Brook Farm to Cedar Mountain in the War of the Great Rebellion, 1861–62*. Revised and enlarged. Boston, MA: Houghton Mifflin & Company, 1885.

———. *History of the Campaign of the Army of Virginia, under John Pope, Brigadier General, U.S.A., Late Major General U.S. Volunteers from Cedar Mountain to Alexandria, 1862*. Boston, MA: Houghton Mifflin & Company, 1880.

————. *A War Diary of Events in the War of the Great Rebellion, 1863–65*. Boston, MA: James R. Osgood & Company, 1882.

Herring, Stephen W. *Framingham: An American Town*. Framingham, MA: Framingham Historical Society, 2000.

Quint, Alonzo H. *The Record of the Second Massachusetts Infantry, 1861–65*. Boston, MA: Chaplain, James P. Walker, 1867.

Scott, Robert N., ed. *The War of the Rebellion: A Compilation of the Official Records of the Union and Confederate Armies*. Series I. Washington, D.C.: Government Printing Office, 1880.

Shouler, William, Adjutant General of the Commonwealth. *History of Massachusetts in the Civil War*. Boston, MA: E.P. Dutton & Company, 1868.

Simon, John Y., ed. *The Papers of Ulysses S. Grant*. Vol. 16. Carbondale: Southern Illinois University Press, 1988.

Temple, Josiah. *History of Framingham, Massachusetts, 1640–1885*. Framingham, MA: Town of Framingham, 1885.

Train, Arthur. *Puritan's Progress*. New York: Charles Scribner & Sons, 1931.

OTHER RESOURCES

Boston Daily Globe online historical database. "Nineteenth Century Newspapers." http://www.gale.cengage.com.

Civil War Correspondence, Diaries, and Journals at the Massachusetts Historical Society, 1754–1926: Bulk 1861–1865, microfilm edition, 29 reels. Papers of George Henry Gordon, Major General, United States Volunteers, 1842–1885, reels 21 through 29, Massachusetts Historical Society.

BIBLIOGRAPHY

Commonwealth of Massachusetts, Art Commission, Massachusetts Statehouse Flag Collection:

1987.360 Presentation National, 2nd Regiment, Massachusetts Volunteer Infantry.
1987.361 Presentation State Color, 2nd Regiment, Massachusetts Volunteer Infantry.
1987.363 State Color, 2nd Regiment, Massachusetts Volunteer Infantry.

Framingham History Center Special Collection, "General George H. Gordon." Framingham, Massachusetts.

Framingham Town Annual Reports, Framingham, Massachusetts.

Massachusetts National Guard Museum and Archives, Salisbury Street, Worcester, Massachusetts.

National Archives Publication Microcopy 688, Record Group 94: Records of the Adjutant General's Office, Entry 243. United States Military Academy Application Papers of Cadets, 1814-669W3: 16/4/2, Box #102, File #88, 1838. Application Papers for George Henry Gordon.

New York Times online historical database. "Nineteenth Century Newspapers." http://www.gale.cengage.com.

Ralph Waldo Emerson Memorial Association Deposit, Houghton Library, Harvard University. Letter, G.H. Gordon to R.W. Emerson, 8 April, 1862.

Images from Massachusetts Historical Society, not to be reproduced without permission:

No Slavery! Fourth of July The Managers of the Anti-Slavery Soc'y. Broadside, Worcester, Massachusetts, printed by Earle & Drew, [1854]. Massachusetts Historical Society.

Gilt ornament taken from the library of the Executive Mansion in Richmond, Virginia, by Brigadier General George H. Gordon. By unidentified maker, unknown date. Artifact number 0198. Massachusetts Historical Society, on loan to Framingham History Center. Photo provided by MHS.

ABOUT THE AUTHOR

Frederic A. Wallace is Framingham's town historian. He has been a volunteer researcher at the Framingham History Center for more than fifteen years and serves on the Framingham Historical Commission. He has published a genealogy, *Ancestors and Descendants of the Rice Brothers of Springfield, Massachusetts, 1704–2004*, and has written many articles on topics relating to the history of Framingham for the center's newsletter.

"With the publication of this work we now have a much better understanding of this remarkable Civil War General. It is a significant contribution to the town's historic record and encourages the Framingham History Center and others to bring Gordon's story to life. Like much of Framingham's Civil War history, his achievements were largely overlooked. Thanks to Town Historian Fred Wallace, Gordon now has the recognition he deserves."

Annie Murphy
Executive Director
Framingham History Center